capital
needs
in the
seventies

Barry Bosworth
James S. Duesenberry
Andrew S. Carron

Brookings Institution

CAPITAL NEEDS
IN THE SEVENTIES

BARRY BOSWORTH
JAMES S. DUESENBERRY
ANDREW S. CARRON

CAPITAL NEEDS
IN THE SEVENTIES

THE BROOKINGS INSTITUTION
Washington, D.C.

Library of Congress Cataloging in Publication Data:
Bosworth, Barry, 1942–
  Capital needs in the seventies.
  Includes bibliographical references.
  1. Capital—United States.   2. Economic forecasting—
United States.   3. United States—Economic conditions—
1961–   1. Duesenberry, James Stemble, 1918–
joint author.   II. Carron, Andrew S., joint author.
III. Title.
HC110.C3B6   332'.041   75-5157
ISBN 0-8157-1031-3

9 8 7 6 5 4 3 2 1

THE BROOKINGS INSTITUTION is an independent organization devoted to nonpartisan research, education, and publication in economics, government, foreign policy, and the social sciences generally. Its principal purposes are to aid in the development of sound public policies and to promote public understanding of issues of national importance.

The Institution was founded on December 8, 1927, to merge the activities of the Institute for Government Research, founded in 1916, the Institute of Economics, founded in 1922, and the Robert Brookings Graduate School of Economics and Government, founded in 1924.

The Board of Trustees is responsible for the general administration of the Institution, while the immediate direction of the policies, program, and staff is vested in the President, assisted by an advisory committee of the officers and staff. The by-laws of the Institution state: "It is the function of the Trustees to make possible the conduct of scientific research, and publication, under the most favorable conditions, and to safeguard the independence of the research staff in the pursuit of their studies and in the publication of the results of such studies. It is not a part of their function to determine, control, or influence the conduct of particular investigations or the conclusions reached."

The President bears final responsibility for the decision to publish a manuscript as a Brookings book. In reaching his judgment on the competence, accuracy, and objectivity of each study, the President is advised by the director of the appropriate research program and weighs the views of a panel of expert outside readers who report to him in confidence on the quality of the work. Publication of a work signifies that it is deemed a competent treatment worthy of public consideration but does not imply endorsement of conclusions or recommendations.

The Institution maintains its position of neutrality on issues of public policy in order to safeguard the intellectual freedom of the staff. Hence interpretations or conclusions in Brookings publications should be understood to be solely those of the authors and should not be attributed to the Institution, to its trustees, officers, or other staff members, or to the organizations that support its research.

1055076

Foreword

In RECENT YEARS, new energy requirements, capacity shortages in many raw material processing industries, and the need for pollution abatement equipment, housing, and mass transportation have intensified the demand for industrial capacity enough to induce fear that the United States is entering an era of severe capital shortage. Some observers have concluded that the shortage will force curtailment of public or private investment programs.

In this study, the authors examine the probable supply of and demand for capital in the remainder of the 1970s. They project total output to 1980 at high employment and estimate the corresponding amount of investment that will be needed in the private economy. These estimates are then compared with an estimate of private saving to determine the federal budget surplus required to make the total available for investment equal to the amount needed.

The study also examines the problems of matching the projected borrowing needs of states and local governments, industrial and commercial enterprises, and households with the funds ordinarily available to such borrowers through the nation's financial intermediaries. Although savings may be adequate, the composition of money flows through the capital markets may exert undue pressure on existing financial institutions and make some reforms desirable.

The authors conclude that the capital needs—though large—will be manageable in an expanding economy with a growing capacity to supply savings. They expect private investment as a share of gross national product to exceed its average level during the 1960s but to be only slightly above the level at which it stood as recently as 1973. Although the growth of private investment demand will require a shift of fiscal policy toward larger budget surpluses, in their view, the requisite surplus at high employment will not be so large as to be unrealistic. In the financial sector, enough money should be available for the public and private investment demand that the authors project—if the federal budget surplus is large enough and if monetary policy is not too restrictive. A relatively easy monetary policy will be necessary, they believe, to enable financial intermediaries to absorb the projected increases in long-term private debt.

The projections of financial flows in this study are based in part on the capital market model devised by Barry Bosworth and James Duesenberry, which was described in their article, "A Flow of Funds Model and Its Implications," *Issues in Federal Debt Management*, Federal Reserve Bank of Boston Conference Series No. 10 (June 1973; Brookings Technical Series Reprint T-005).

This study developed from a project on capital market behavior financed by a grant from the Ford Foundation. Barry Bosworth is a member of the staff of the Brookings Economic Studies program. James S. Duesenberry is professor of economics at Harvard University and a member of the Brookings associated staff. Andrew Carron was a Brookings research assistant when this volume was prepared.

The authors express their appreciation for the research help of John Farmer and Eric Pookrum. Evelyn Taylor provided secretarial assistance. The manuscript was edited by Elizabeth H. Cross; its factual content was verified by Evelyn P. Fisher.

The views expressed here are solely those of the authors and should not be ascribed to the institutions with which they are affiliated, or to the trustees, officers, and other staff members of the Brookings Institution or to the Ford Foundation.

KERMIT GORDON
President

April 1975
Washington, D.C.

Contents

Tables

Figures

CHAPTER ONE

Introduction

DURING the postwar period the American economy has demonstrated an unparalleled capacity to produce goods and services of all kinds. In spite of periods of inflation and occasional recessions, living standards have risen almost continuously. At the same time the volume of saving has provided for a continuous upgrading and renovation of industrial and commercial capital as well as for new plants and equipment for a growing work force. In the public sector the demands of a vastly expanded educational system have been met with little strain and 40,000 miles of interstate highways have been built. Nonetheless, capital requirements, far from being satisfied, are greater than ever. The demand for industrial capital is intensified by the need to find new sources of energy, by insufficient capacity in many industries processing raw materials, and by the need for pollution abatement. Widely accepted national housing goals mean that 25 million new homes must be built in ten years. In the public sector large amounts of capital will be required for water treatment and mass transit.

Adding up the capital necessary for all the projects that either promise a profitable private return or appear high on someone's list of social priorities for the rest of the seventies yields a total of over $2 trillion. Such calculations suggest that, as one writer put it, "we may not be able to afford the future." Some capital market Cassandras predict a large-scale capital shortage which will require high real rates of interest, sharp increases in tax rates, and a scaling down of capital programs for social improvement in such fields as housing and pollution control.

Some of the gloom is readily dispelled by annualizing multiyear capital requirement estimates and recognizing that in a growing economy the

1

capacity to produce and to save will increase by 50 percent by the end of the decade. Moreover, while new capital demands have arisen, existing capital requirements in some areas are declining. The classroom shortage of a few years ago is gone. The interstate highway program is nearing completion. These observations do not mean that there is no problem, but they do suggest that the dimensions of the problem can only be understood by a careful analysis of the balance between the growing demand for capital and the growing resources of the economy.

This paper reports the results of a study, begun in 1973 before the energy squeeze, of the probable demand for capital—public and private—and of the potential supply of capital from 1974 to 1980. Is it possible to provide industrial capital for an expanding economy, develop new sources of energy, achieve the national housing goal, and meet commitments for public and private expenditures for pollution abatement and transit facilities? Or must higher tax rates, underfunded programs, and congested capital markets be expected? Our answer is that we can afford the future, but just barely. Although investment needs will represent a higher share of total output than in the past decade, they can be met by a moderate adjustment of fiscal and monetary policies.

Our objective is not so much to forecast what will actually happen as to provide a basis for judging both the implications of the fiscal and monetary policy decisions that will have to be made in the next few years and whether existing investment programs and public expenditure policies have already overcommitted resources. We begin in chapter 2 by examining the sources of potential output to 1980, and then direct attention to the special factors affecting the growth of housing demand, public and private investment in the physical environment, and investment in energy. We survey the prospective growth of state and local expenditures, demand for business investment, and existing federal expenditure commitments, and we estimate private consumption. These pieces are then drawn together to produce estimates of private saving and investment and of the amount of federal surplus required to balance the excess of private investment over private saving. This leads to estimates of the amount available for federal tax reduction or new expenditure programs.

The problems of financing the projected levels of investment are reviewed in chapter 3. The borrowing required for residential construction, state and local government capital formation, and business investment is derived from the nonfinancial projections of chapter 2. These are combined with the saving flows of the remaining sectors to determine the composition of credit market obligations by issuer and holder for a specific set of fiscal and monetary policy assumptions. Finally, we examine briefly the potential effect on U.S. capital markets of the sharp rise in the world price of oil.

Summary of the Estimates

The estimates indicate that with normal growth and without unusual sacrifices the economy will be able to meet the capital demands that can reasonably be projected for the remainder of the decade. At the same time, very careful fiscal management will be required to avoid a capital market crunch or a renewal of inflationary demand pressures (on top of the cost-push that is likely to persist for several years).

Our projections suggest that once the economy returns to a full employment growth path the rate of capital formation should exceed the rates achieved during the 1960s in relative as well as absolute terms. Gross private domestic capital formation for 1980 is projected at 15.8 percent of the gross national product, about the same as the average for the 1950s and for the year 1973, but well above the average for the 1960s.

Business investment as a percentage of GNP is expected to be higher than in the 1950s, but the share going to residential construction is expected to fall off. Two million housing starts a year (exclusive of mobile homes) will meet the national housing goal while absorbing a declining share of a rising GNP.

The projected rise in business investment, though not spectacular, implies a significant shift in the long-run direction of fiscal policy. At full employment, private investment is likely to exceed private saving; accordingly, a full employment surplus rather than a deficit will be appropriate.

Our estimates of the required budget surplus are greatly affected by the choice of an unemployment target. The basic estimates use a conventional 4 percent target because many estimates of full employment revenues (including the estimates in the annual Brookings publication *Setting National Priorities,* to which ours are linked) are based on this assumed rate of resource utilization. Since many observers doubt that inflation can be controlled with an unemployment rate as low as 4 percent, after developing the projection on a 4 percent basis, we show adjustments to 5 percent. The change makes a good deal of difference. A one percentage point rise in the unemployment rate would reduce GNP by about 2 percent. In 1980 that would amount to $40 billion (at 1973 prices). The required full employment surplus would be about half of 1 percent of GNP with a 4 percent unemployment target, but would have to exceed 1 percent with a 5 percent target.

While our estimates of capital requirements may appear low compared to the estimates—or rhetoric—of people who are alarmed by the implications of the energy squeeze, others will find our estimates unduly high. Recent studies of corporate profits indicate that rates of return on capital have been declining for some years and that the decline is not merely cyclical. One, of course, encounters many difficulties in measuring returns on capital, particularly in an era of inflation. For example, corrections must be made for inventory profits and for the difference between historical cost and replacement cost depreciation. However, a study by William Nordhaus shows that, regardless of how these corrections are made, there has been a downward trend in the rates of return on capital.[1] Some economists believe that falling rates of return mean that investment demand is likely to be weak in the next few years. Other things being equal, it is reasonable to expect a relative increase in the supply of capital to reduce current average profits and also the marginal return on new capital. A decline in average profits seems to imply a decline in expected marginal returns, and therefore a decline in capital formation or a need for improving investment incentives (through lower interest rates or more favorable tax treatment). While recent discussion has centered on an anticipated shortage of savings, the declining trend of profits leads some observers to argue that the estimate of capital "needs" has been greatly inflated.

However, there are many factors that can cause the marginal returns on new capital to rise while the average returns are falling. The most obvious concerns a significant innovation in an industry with free entry. The entry of new firms with new capital using the innovation will alter the supply; this will reduce prices and lower returns to the old firms, and average returns will be lower than before while the return on the new capital is high. The gap will persist until all the old capital has been replaced by new and

1. William D. Nordhaus, "The Falling Share of Profits," *Brookings Papers on Economic Activity* (1:1974), pp. 169–208.

the price has fallen to its new equilibrium. Shifts in demand will produce similar results.

A change in competitive structure, such as reduction or elimination of entry barriers, may have a like effect. During the postwar period the structure of international competition has changed greatly as a result of both trade liberalization and the rapid industrial development of such countries as Germany and Japan. This has intensified competition and limited profits for at least some sectors of the American economy, particularly since the rate of inflation accelerated in the United States. In addition, government pressure was applied to hold down prices in many basic industries from 1966 to 1968. A brief period of freedom in 1969 was followed by recession in 1970–71 and then by price controls from August 1971 to April 1974. All this seems consistent with the view that the rate of return on new capital can be expected to be high—at least with full employment —in spite of some years of declining average rates of return on existing capital. That view is also supported by the high rate of capital formation during 1973 and 1974 and the plans for further expansion that were made in the first part of 1974.

Another problem is that capital formation in 1975 will probably fall below the rate achieved in 1974 in real terms, although there may be some expansion in dollar amounts. It seems clear that 1975 will be a year of high unemployment and considerable excess capacity. In the short run, then, the outlook is for weak capital demand. The realism of our projections thus depends crucially on the assumption that the economy will soon get onto a growth path that leads it back to, say, 5 percent unemployment.

Several factors are responsible for the weak demand of 1974 and 1975. First, the sharp rise in short-term interest rates brought the housing industry almost to a halt by choking off the supply of funds to mortgage lending institutions. Second, the federal budget became increasingly restrictive because dollar expenditures were not raised from the levels projected in early 1974 while revenues continued to swell with inflation. Third, the rise in oil prices represented a loss of real income to consumers, reducing their expenditures while the recipients were not spending the proceeds. To a lesser degree the shift of income to farmers, which accounted for part of the rise in the personal saving rate in early 1974, had a depressive effect. All these factors sapped consumers' confidence and further weakened consumer demand, especially for automobiles.

While these short-run dynamic factors change the immediate outlook for capital formation, they do not imply a lasting change. If the economy is to return to full employment it must grow much more rapidly from 1976 to 1980 than in our original projections, which assumed a fairly steady growth from 1974 on. Total real capital requirements would be about the same in either case, although capital requirements at the end of the decade might be somewhat higher than our estimates to make up for some loss of capital formation in 1974–75.

In the meantime, with the economy operating substantially below full employment, inadequate saving is not a problem. In fact, the problem is just the reverse: private saving exceeds private investment. Deficits generated by the federal government do not reduce private investment in such circumstances. The immediate impact is to use resources that would otherwise be idle and ultimately to promote recovery. Thus, in periods of recession, an expansionary fiscal policy combined with the appropriate degree of monetary ease will not crowd out private investment. On the contrary, the quicker the recession is halted, the sooner the recovery in private investment and the greater the contribution toward the alleviation of long-run capital shortages.

Inflation, Fiscal Policy, and the Transition to Full Employment

The prospects for achieving a long-term balance between saving and investment for federal expenditures and tax policy depend on (1) existing commitments in the federal budget, (2) the impact of inflation on federal and state and local revenues and program costs, and (3) the difficulty of providing a short-run stimulus to a depressed economy without undertaking excessive commitments for the longer term.

Our original projections were based on the assumption that inflation would gradually diminish from the 6 percent rate of 1973 to 3 percent by about 1978. These projections, which now appear optimistic, led us to conclude that the full employment surplus required by the end of the decade could be achieved with current federal tax rates and only a very limited amount of new expenditure. Present legislation and the current administration defense posture would produce a rapid increase in federal expenditures even if no legislation authorizing new spending were passed. On the other hand, federal revenues normally expand in a growing economy. Inflation increases revenues even more rapidly than it drives up expenditures because the "bracket effect" raises the average effective income tax rate. Our original projections indicated that by 1980 federal revenues would have risen to $60 billion to $80 billion more than the amount required to meet present federal commitments. The higher figure would be achieved if unemployment were held to 4 percent; the lower figure corresponds to a more realistic 5 percent unemployment target and a correspondingly lower GNP.

At first glance the built-in fiscal dividend (more realistically, an inflation dividend) appeared to allow for large new expenditures. But the projections also showed that state and local governments would need around $30 billion of transfers from the federal government. Of the remainder, a substantial amount would have to be reserved to offset the excess of private saving over private investment. Thus whittled down, the amount of unallocated resources available for new expenditure consistent with a 5 percent unemployment target appeared to be as low as $10 billion (1973 prices). A 4 percent unemployment target would permit a much larger increase in federal expenditures, but would also require major changes in labor and product markets.

Since the original projections were made, the oil crisis and the resurgence of inflation have made our dollar calculations obsolete though they leave most of the real magnitudes intact. In one important respect, however, a rise in the rate of inflation affects the real magnitudes in the system as well as the nominal ones. As already noted, inflation tends to push federal revenues up faster than expenditures. We estimate that a 1 percent increase in the GNP deflator would raise the cost of a given federal program by about 1 percent. A 1 percent rise in the price level would increase federal revenues from a given real GNP by about 1.2 percent.

The discussion of resource availability in chapter 2 states that, to provide for (1) the present heavy commitments in the federal budget, (2) the needs of state and local governments, and (3) an adequate full employment surplus by 1980, the public will have to accept some increase in effective tax rates and a corresponding decline in the share of consumption in total GNP. The calculations in chapter 2 show that the required increase in effective tax rates would be automatically produced by the modest 4.5 percent average inflation rate assumed there, but the calculations also show that there would be relatively little left over. We therefore assumed no adjustment of nominal tax rates.

If the rate of inflation exceeds 4.5 percent a year, effective tax rates and full employment revenues would be higher than assumed here. This would allow Congress and the administration to choose between new expenditure programs and tax rate reductions to offset the additional increase in the budget surplus. It seems reasonable to suppose that some reduction in nominal tax rates will be needed to prevent a further rise in effective tax rates as the inflation proceeds. An extra degree of flexibility in fiscal policy could be gained by choosing the timing of such tax rate adjustments to meet short-term stabilization needs.

Measures to ease fiscal and monetary policy could get the economy back onto its long-term growth path in two or three years with minimal danger that inflationary demand pressures would be generated either by too high a rate of growth or by overshooting the ultimate unemployment rate target. To reduce unemployment to 5 percent will require that real GNP grow for some time at a faster rate than its normal 4 percent. For example, even if real GNP grew at 5.5 percent, it would take six years or more to bring unemployment down to 5 percent.

If we assume (perhaps too optimistically) that the appropriate fiscal and monetary steps are taken, our estimates of capital formation and saving requirements in real terms remain virtually the same. The average growth rate of GNP would be unchanged, although the actual growth would be lower in 1975 and higher in later years than originally assumed. Requirements for housing and business investment will be only somewhat affected by the 1974–75 shortfall in housing and the projected shortfall in business fixed investment in 1975, but the basic message about long-term fiscal policy remains the same.

While we could have attempted to make new projections that would appear more realistic in light of recent price developments, it is impossible to predict the course of inflation. Fortunately, for our general purpose a precise prediction of the inflation rate is unnecessary. Most of the current dollar estimates in our projections can be adjusted if necessary without altering the real magnitudes.

The absolute rate of inflation enters the calculations in a different way in the financial discussion of chapter 3. Our projections there assume a fiscal policy that provides enough saving, public and private, to equal the projected initial volume of investment at full employment, and a 4.5 percent long-term real interest rate. With a 3 percent inflation rate, this implies a 7.5 percent nominal long-term rate and a short-term rate of around 6.5 percent for Treasury bills. In chapter 3 we also assume that the Federal Reserve provides enough bank reserves to produce the required short-term rate, and we then examine the distribution of different types of securities by issuer and holder. With the decline in the outstanding volume of federal securities, there will be a decline in the overall supply of liquid assets. Otherwise, no major problems appear.

A higher rate of inflation implies a higher level of short-term interest rates. Therefore the thrift institutions might have difficulties because their ability to compete for deposits depends on earnings based on mortgages acquired in the past. These problems also are discussed in detail in chapter 3.

Conclusion

Although expensionary fiscal and monetary policies may be needed in the short run to counter high unemployment and inadequate real demand, we can foresee for the long run unusually strong demands for capital and the need for a fiscal policy that yields a substantial full employment surplus. The longer-term fiscal outlook is dominated by three circumstances: the large existing commitments for increased expenditures already built into the federal budget, the necessity for providing additional assistance to state and local governments to meet social priorities, and the fact that inflation increases federal revenues faster than program costs.

The responsiveness of the federal revenue system is the key to resolving the apparent inconsistency between the short-run and long-run objectives of fiscal policy. The average effective tax rate rises with inflation, and this will impose an inflation-induced fiscal drag on the economy. This would happen even if dollar expenditures were increased to keep pace with inflation. It is therefore possible to contemplate a substantial fiscal stimulus to reverse the 1974–75 recession and still plan for a full employment surplus at the end of the decade, when capital demands will be much stronger.

CHAPTER TWO

Claims on Output
in the Seventies

IN THIS CHAPTER we examine the supply of available resources and the potential claims on them, through 1980, for their effects on the whole economy rather than on individual sectors. Others have calculated the costs of specific investment programs such as housing, pollution abatement, and energy development. But these analyses are of limited help in evaluating project feasibility unless placed in a more general framework which takes into account the total quantity of resources available and the competing claims. For example, projections of revenues and expenditures five years into the future are now a regular part of the administration's federal budget proposals. The resulting budget surplus or deficit, however, can be a misleading indicator of the funds available for new spending —unless one assumes that a balanced budget is the right fiscal policy. Determining the appropriate budget balance depends on the strength of demand in other sectors of the economy in relation to the total available supply of resources. Thus, if high levels of private consumption and investment are anticipated, the full amount of a projected surplus would not be available for tax reductions or budget initiatives.

Here particular attention is devoted to areas requiring substantial amounts of capital investment. The cost estimates for specific programs are based on existing studies where possible, adjusted for a consistent projection of the inflation rate.

Projections of Resource Availability

Real gross national product is projected to grow slightly faster during the remainder of the 1970s than during the 1960s. Output must expand by 4.3 percent annually between 1973 and 1980 if jobs are to be found for new labor force entrants and if the goal of 4 percent unemployment is to be realized by 1980. As shown in table 2-1 the total labor force will continue to expand by about 2 percent a year. A more rapid growth in the working-age population than in the 1960s—resulting from the many postwar babies having reached young adulthood—is partially offset by a less rapid rise in the labor force participation rate of women.[1] Employment growth will become more rapid in the middle of the decade as the economy recovers from the 1974–75 recession. Most of this increased employment will be concentrated in the private sector, since federal employment is projected to remain constant and growth in state and local employment is lower than in the 1960s because of a drop in elementary school enrollment.

The growth of labor productivity in the private sector has increased by about 3 percent a year in the postwar period, and this trend is expected to continue. The shift from agriculture to higher-productivity industrial jobs, however, will be of minimal importance, and the decrease in annual hours per worker is likely to continue at the rate of the last five years.

The projection for the rate of inflation is more uncertain than that for real output. We have assumed that the rate of inflation will decline steadily through 1980.[2] The projected average annual rate of increase in the GNP deflator for the private sector is 4.4 percent (4.7 percent for the overall GNP deflator) between 1973 and 1980. The GNP deflator for the government sector is assumed to rise in line with private wage rates. The 3 percent inflation rate reached by 1980 falls between the 2.4 percent rate of the 1960s and the 4.2 percent rate of 1970–73. We have thus assumed

1. The projections in this section rely heavily on four papers from a U.S. Bureau of Labor Statistics study of the economy in 1985, especially one by Ronald E. Kutscher, "Projections of GNP, Income, Output, and Employment," *Monthly Labor Review,* vol. 96 (December 1973), pp. 27–42. The other articles appear on pp. 3–26 of the same issue. We have projected a larger total labor force for 1980, which reflects a greater rise in the labor force participation rate of women, but a lower trend growth in output per employee in the private sector. Our results give real output estimates for 1980 that are almost identical with those of the BLS study.

2. These projections, begun in late 1973, do not reflect the sharp rise in the inflation rate in 1974.

Table 2-1. *U.S. Labor Force, Man-Hours, and Output, Selected Years, 1960–80*

Description	Actual			Projected		Average annual rate of change		
	1960	1970	1973	1977	1980	1960–70	1970–73	1973–80
Labor force (millions)								
Total	72.1	85.9	91.0	98.1	102.9	1.8	1.9	1.8
Unemployed	3.9	4.1	4.3	4.5	4.0	0.5	1.6	-1.0
Employment (persons concept)[a]	68.3	81.8	86.7	93.6	98.9	1.8	2.0	1.9
Employment (jobs concept)[a]	71.8	86.8	91.3	99.0	104.8	1.9	1.7	2.0
Government[b]	10.2	14.7	15.1	16.6	17.9	3.7	0.9	2.5
Private	61.6	72.1	76.2	82.4	86.9	1.6	1.9	1.9
Private sector								
Average man-hours per worker	2,067	1,969	1,969	1,934	1,920	-0.5	-0.1	-0.3
Total man-hours (billions)	127.3	142.0	149.4	159.4	166.8	1.1	1.7	1.6
GNP per man-hour (1973 dollars)	5.14	6.86	7.64	8.55	9.33	2.9	3.7	2.9
Gross national product								
Total (billions of 1973 dollars)	758.0	1,118.4	1,289.1	1,524.7	1,730.2	4.0	4.9	4.3
Government[b]	104.1	144.0	147.5	161.7	173.8	3.3	0.8	2.4
Private	653.9	974.4	1,141.6	1,363.0	1,556.4	4.1	5.4	4.5
Total (billions of current dollars)	503.7	977.1	1,289.1	1,896.8	2,387.5	6.9	9.7	9.2
Government[b]	47.5	114.7	147.5	221.2	286.6	9.2	8.8	10.0
Private	456.3	862.4	1,141.6	1,675.6	2,100.9	6.6	9.8	9.1
Price deflator (1973 = 100)	66.5	87.9	100.0	124.4	138.0	2.8	4.4	4.7
Government[b]	46.0	80.0	100.0	136.8	164.9	5.7	7.7	7.4
Private	69.8	88.5	100.0	122.9	135.0	2.4	4.2	4.4

Sources: U.S. Department of Commerce, *Survey of Current Business*, vol. 54, February 1974 and earlier issues; Bureau of Labor Statistics, *Monthly Labor Review*, vol. 96 (December 1973), pp. 8–42; and authors' projections. Figures are rounded.
a. Employment (persons concept) is the number of people holding jobs. Employment (jobs concept) is the number of jobs held; if people hold more than one job they are counted more than once.
b. Military and civilian federal government and state and local governments.

that the United States will extricate itself from its current problems without a full renewal of the wage-price spiral of 1969–71 and that agriculture prices will decline slightly in relative terms.

Since many of the detailed projections that follow are made in real terms, the inflation projections are not crucial to all aspects of this study, and the assumed 4 percent unemployment rate is probably unrealistic. They are adopted here so that we can arrive at a benchmark estimate of total available resources. These inflation-unemployment assumptions facilitate comparison with previous studies of specific sectors of the economy, studies that have been used as sources for many of the individual projections which we have aggregated into a larger survey. They are optimistic estimates, however, in view of the current chaotic state of the economy. Therefore, in later sections of this chapter and in chapter 3 some implications of a less favorable inflation-unemployment trade-off are examined.

Housing

For over four decades the federal government has actively sought to increase the quantity and quality of housing in the United States. Attempts to achieve this objective are reflected in the income tax code, the regulation of financial institutions, and the rapid proliferation of special purpose programs. Collectively, these efforts define a multifaceted national housing policy. Coincident with this growth of federal government activity has been a significant improvement in housing conditions. Yet in recent years increasing concern has been expressed about a broad range of problems: discrimination, the adequacy and stability of total production, minimum standards, and costs.

Housing finance is only one dimension of housing policy, but rising interest costs and recent severe swings in mortgage availability have focused concern on this area. Financial market conditions have a major effect on two national housing goals: providing adequate total financing for the housing needs of the 1970s and minimizing cyclical disruptions in housing finance.[3] Thus housing needs for the rest of this decade are examined here to provide a basis for a projection of residential mortgage demand.

3. A more thorough discussion of the broader issues of national housing policy can be found in studies such as Henry J. Aaron, *Shelter and Subsidies: Who Benefits from Federal Housing Policies?* (Brookings Institution, 1972), and Frank deLeeuw, "What Should U.S. Housing Policies Be?" in American Finance Association, *Papers and Proceedings of the Thirty-second Annual Meeting, 1973* (*Journal of Finance*, vol. 29, May 1974), pp. 699–721.

The Demand for Housing in the 1970s

The Housing Act of 1949 called for the "realization as soon as feasible of the goal of a decent home and a suitable living environment for every American family." The Housing and Urban Development Act of 1968 went further, declaring a goal of 26 million new and rehabilitated housing units during fiscal 1969–78. This total was to include 6 million units for low- and moderate-income families.

Subsequent interpretation yielded a goal of 25 million new units (5 million subsidized) and 1 million subsidized rehabilitations. By 1970 the administration had further apportioned the 25 million new units into 21 million conventional single and multifamily units and 4 million mobile homes —a category of housing previously excluded.

THE GOAL OF 25 MILLION. The adequacy of the ten-year housing goal can be partially evaluated by looking at the pattern of demand for the rest of this decade. Housing requirements arise from (1) increases in the total number of households caused by population growth and other sociological factors, (2) upgrading the quality of the housing stock through replacement of substandard units, and (3) providing low-cost housing to low-income people through an increase in the vacancy rate. These do not constitute a complete demand function, but they do describe the basis for the 1968 housing goals. In addition, the demand for housing is affected by demographic composition, relative prices, real income, and general monetary conditions.

Housing needs for the 1970s are shown in table 2-2. Household formation is projected to continue for the rest of this decade at the high rates of the late 1960s and early 1970s. New home construction has always exceeded household formation to allow for the removal of old units and for shifts in the geographical distribution of the population. However, a much larger gap between production and household formation is implied by the 1968 housing goal. In addition to substantially increasing removals, the government hopes to raise the vacancy rate, thereby easing supply problems and holding down rents. The higher vacancy rate also reflects a growing trend toward vacation homes, which are unoccupied much of the year.

The projections of the Department of Housing and Urban Development (HUD) called for constructing 10.5 million units during fiscal years 1969–73, with the remaining 14.5 million to be built from 1974 to 1978.[4]

4. *First Annual Report on National Housing Goals, Message from the President of the United States,* H. Doc. 91-63, 91 Cong. 1 sess. (1969), and subsequent editions (1970–73).

Table 2-2. *Change in the Housing Stock, 1950–80*

Millions of units

Description	1950	1960	1970	1980
Housing stock				
Occupied units	43.0	53.3	64.0	79.5
Vacant units[a]	3.2	5.0	6.2	9.7
Total	46.1	58.3	70.2	89.2
Vacancy rate (percent)	6.9	8.6	8.8	10.9
Change from preceding decade				
Units added	n.a.	16.9	18.6	27.0
New construction	n.a.	15.0	17.2	25.8
Other[b]	n.a.	1.9	1.4	1.2
Units removed[c]	n.a.	4.5	6.7	8.0
Net change	n.a.	12.3	11.9	19.0

Sources: 1950, U.S. Bureau of the Census, *U.S. Census of Housing, 1960*, vol. 4, *Components of Inventory Change*, Final Report HC(4), pt. 1A, no. 1, *1950–1959 Components* (1962), pp. 22, 26; 1960, 1970, Bureau of the Census, *Census of Housing, 1970, Components of Inventory Change*, Final Report HC(4)-1 (1973), pp. 1-10, 1-17; 1980, authors' projections. Stocks for 1980 are based on the 1973 estimate of households, plus annual growth projected, in Bureau of the Census, *Current Population Reports*, Series P-25, no. 476, "Demographic Projections for the United States" (1972). Removals are based on the average rates for the 1950s and 1960s for units except mobile homes, which are based on rates for the 1960s only. Figures are rounded.
n.a. Not available.
a. Includes seasonal units (vacation homes).
b. Conversions from group and nonresidential quarters and miscellaneous additions.
c. Demolitions, mergers, or conversions to group or nonresidential use, units unfit for habitation, and units destroyed by fire or flood.

During the first five years actual construction of 11.6 million units exceeded the government's projections and the 13.4 million goal for fiscal years 1974–78 seems well within reach despite the relatively few (2.2 million) units produced in fiscal 1974. This would mean an annual rate of about 2.8 million units for fiscal 1975–78, about half a million higher than the 1969–74 average—which included two years when fewer than 2 million new units were produced—but lower than the rate for 1972, when more than 3 million units were built.

Several considerations lessen the apparent success to date in meeting the 1968 goal. HUD projected an increasing rate of construction, peaking in 1976–77, although the Census Bureau has forecast no increase in the rate of household formation. A constant rate of housing production throughout the decade might have been more realistic in view of the substantial initial demand shown by the very low vacancy rate. In that context, attaining 47 percent of the goal in the first half of the period may be viewed as only modest progress. Second, the much lower production rate during the credit squeeze of 1973–74 necessitates a relatively rapid recovery and high production for the last three years of the planning period.

Table 2-3. *Net Household Formation and Composition of Housing Production, Selected Periods, 1956–80*

Thousands, annual average

		New units			
Period	Net household formation	Single-family dwellings	Multi-family dwellings[a]	Mobile homes	Total
1956–65	929	975	471	133	1,579
1969–73[b]	1,491	1,043	853	495	2,392
1974–78[c]	1,450	1,196	900	571	2,667
1980[c]	1,450	1,275	875	575	2,725

Sources: Household formation calculated from Bureau of the Census, *Current Population Reports*, Series P-20, no. 251, "Households and Families, by Type: March 1973" (1973); housing units calculated from Bureau of the Census, *Construction Reports*, C20, "Housing Starts," various issues; 1974–80, authors' projections. Figures are rounded.
a. Includes public housing.
b. Estimated by authors from partial data.
c. Projected.

A final issue in assessing how well the 1968 goal is being met is the substitution of mobile homes for conventional dwellings. The federal government has projected 4 million new mobile homes during the decade, although recent growth in that segment of the housing market and the 2.6 million units produced in the first five years suggest that 5 million is more likely. Mobile homes offer significant cost advantages over conventional units. They are particularly attractive for the retired, a rapidly growing segment of the population. Their lack of durability, however, generates greater demand for replacements, and they may conflict with local land use planning.

PROJECTIONS TO 1980. We used a projection of housing starts for the rest of the 1970s that is consistent with the goal of 25 million new units. However, the composition shown in table 2-3 is considerably different from what was originally visualized, as mobile homes and multifamily units represent a far larger proportion of total starts. The projections assume that the tight credit conditions end with 1974 and that there is a sharp upturn in 1975 with an average annual rate of 2.7 million new units from 1974 through 1980. While this level is slightly below the average for 1971–73, it is high in relation to net household formation when judged by historical standards.

In the last half of the 1960s there was a shift in the distribution of households toward the younger age groups. In addition, the costs of both sites and construction rose at faster rates than the general price level. These are

Table 2-4. *Housing Starts and Value of Residential Construction, Selected Years, 1960–80*

Year	Housing starts[a] (thousands)	Value of residential construction (billions)	
		1973 dollars	Current dollars
1960	1,296	37.3	22.9
1965	1,510	40.7	27.3
1970	1,469	37.9	31.9
1973	2,058	58.0	58.0
1977[b]	2,225	57.3	75.8
1980[b]	2,150	56.3	83.5

Sources: *Survey of Current Business*, various issues; and authors' projections.
a. Excludes mobile homes.
b. Projected.

among the identifiable factors that led to the sharp increase in multifamily housing starts and mobile home shipments. For the rest of this decade, the demographic shifts will be less pronounced and a stable allocation of total new units can be expected.

If monetary conditions improve, the goal of 25 million units appears to be a reasonable and attainable aggregate target, although conventional starts will be well below the level anticipated in 1968. Our estimates do not indicate the need for a major expansion of home-building capacity to compensate for the drop in the annual rate of production from the high output of 1971 and 1972.

Building costs have risen rapidly in recent years, averaging 5.1 percent a year from 1965 to 1972 and 9 percent in 1973. This is primarily the result of large increases in the wages of construction workers and in the cost of materials in the 1972–73 boom. We project that these increases will slow down and rise more in accordance with the general price level. The projected slight rise in the real value per unit is in line with the trend of the previous ten years. The resulting estimates of real construction outlays, as shown in table 2-4, remain below the 1973 peak level for the rest of the 1970s. However, rising costs result in substantial current dollar increases.

Investing in the Physical Environment

Environmental issues have become a major concern in both the private and government sectors, not only because of the intense public interest they have engendered, but also because of their potentially heavy demand on capital budgets. In many areas, investments will be made that will bring little tangible return to the individual investor. Private returns may even be negative, as in the case of the antipollution device that increases fuel consumption or decreases output. The size and distribution of these investments become critically important on the financial side; at the same time, attempts to deal with environmental problems are handicapped by the pressures of population and industrial growth, resource scarcity, potential irreversibility, and visible public concern.

The planning of environmental programs carries the additional burden of uncertainty about costs and needs. Government agencies, such as the Environmental Protection Agency (EPA), the Council on Environmental Quality (CEQ), and the Federal Energy Administration, have begun formulating guidelines. But there are still questions of timing, feasibility, and the costs of compliance, as well as trade-offs between capital costs and operating costs. In this section we will examine projected spending levels based on government guidelines and present industry and other private estimates of future capital requirements.

Environmental planning is not confined to the installation of pollution control devices on smokestacks and in sewer systems. It also embraces transportation systems, conservation and development, and energy production. These are all interrelated, although efforts so far have not reached the level of planning for the environmental system as a whole. Some of the connections—as between energy and transportation, or transportation and pollution—have been explored. By and large, however, planning has developed most fully only in discrete areas. The following analysis will describe the expenditures thought to be required; these data should give an indication of the future demands on capital markets.

The Public Sector

Governments have traditionally been responsible for a variety of capital-intensive programs. Since federal projects are financed out of current revenues, they have no direct implications for credit markets. Thus this analysis is limited to public works financed through state and local governments. In some cases, federal grants-in-aid are a factor in this financing, but they will be discussed in a later section.

Capital investment by state and local governments goes for a variety of

Table 2-5. *Capital Expenditures of State and Local Governments, by Sector, Selected Years, 1965–80*

Billions of 1973 dollars

Expenditure category	1965[a]	1973[b]	Projected 1977	Projected 1980
Construction in small-growth sectors				
Housing and redevelopment	0.8	0.8	0.8	0.8
Schools	7.8	6.6	6.6	6.3
Highways	12.1	10.2	10.3	11.0
Conservation and related development	1.0	0.4	0.8	0.8
Hospitals	0.7	0.8	1.1	1.1
Other buildings	2.4	3.4	4.0	4.3
Subtotal	24.8	22.2	23.6	24.3
Construction in large-growth sectors				
Sewer systems	1.8	2.0	5.7	5.4
Water supply systems	2.3	1.1	2.0	2.4
Other[c]	2.3	2.4	2.9	3.3
Subtotal	6.4	5.5	10.6	11.0
Total construction	**31.2**	**27.7**	**34.2**	**35.4**
Equipment	**4.3**	**6.7**	**7.8**	**8.8**

Sources: Bureau of the Census, *Construction Reports—C30—* "Value of New Construction Put in Place," various issues; *Survey of Current Business*, February 1974; and authors' projections. Figures are rounded.
a. Estimated from current-dollar data, using public sector construction deflators.
b. Preliminary.
c. Includes transit systems, airports, and electric light and power systems, not buildings.

projects (see table 2-5). Real demand in most of these areas is not expected to increase very much. No new major public housing projects are foreseen and the drop in elementary school enrollment will reduce the construction of new schools almost to the replacement rate. The federal interstate highway program is nearing completion, indicating that real expenditures for highways and streets will increase only slightly, if at all. Conservation and development investment has remained at a constant real level for many years, and there is no indication of growth in this relatively small area. New hospitals and other buildings will be built at about the rate of population increase.

There are three "growth" sectors in state and local construction that may affect credit-market financing. These are sewer systems, water resource projects, and miscellaneous construction (which would include mass transit systems). Despite the increase in the real rate of expenditures for water resources (4.8 percent annual compound rate from 1972 to

1980), the amounts are small and the increases are in line with recent trends. It is financing for new sewer systems and mass transit projects that will have the greatest impact on credit markets.

SEWER SYSTEMS. The Federal Water Pollution Control Act Amendments of 1972 set water quality standards for waste treatment facilities and provided federal grants to assist state and local governments in procuring the necessary systems. In most cases, this means secondary treatment plants, which remove 85 to 90 percent of the damaging pollutants. Federal grants equal to 75 percent of the cost of eligible projects were provided for in the act, although the total allocation has been a major source of dispute between the President and Congress.

Estimates of real needs have been made by the EPA. In 1971 a survey of communities yielded an estimate of $18.1 billion for treatment plants, while an economic and engineering cost model the same year produced a $14.4 billion estimate (both in 1971 dollars). A later (1973) EPA estimate, based on a wider range of plants, gave a revised figure of $22.8 billion (1973 dollars). The 1972 act also made some intercepting sewers, force mains, and pumping stations eligible for matching federal funds; the 1973 EPA estimate gave $13.8 billion as the cost of these additional systems.[5]

Some categories of waste treatment systems are not covered by the 1972 act. These include rehabilitation of sewers to correct infiltration and inflow, construction of certain new collecting and intercepting sewers, and correction of overflows from combined sanitary and storm sewers. The total estimated cost of these "optional" improvements is $24.1 billion, giving a grand total of $60.7 billion for all improvements.[6]

For the purposes of this study, however, it will be most useful to determine the capital expenditures that must be made by state and local governments during the current decade to meet the requirements of the 1972 act as well as more stringent local requirements where they exist. The estimate of state and local capital investment for water pollution control published in the 1973 CEQ annual report is $47.2 billion (in 1972 dollars) for fiscal years 1972–81. This includes a small amount of private invest-

5. These data are from Environmental Protection Agency, *The Economics of Clean Water* (1972), vol. 1, pp. 114, 127, and statistics in *Environmental Quality, The Fourth Annual Report of the Council on Environmental Quality* (1973), chap. 3.

6. The total of $60.7 billion is composed of $22.8 billion for treatment plants, $13.8 billion for transmission systems, and $24.1 billion for categories excluded from the 1972 act.

ment and presumably takes into account both needs and the feasibility of meeting them. Recently, CEQ and others have estimated that spending by municipalities in 1972–80 will be $38.8 billion (1972 dollars). The difference between this figure and the published $47.2 billion estimate mentioned above is attributable primarily to the shorter time involved, and also to differences of opinion about feasibility and the immediacy of needs.

Since the stormy enactment of the Water Pollution Control Act Amendments, new questions have been raised about the capacity of the industry that will build the treatment facilities. From 1965 to 1971 the real value of sewer construction was approximately constant, but the federal program calls for an annual capacity increase of about 30 percent (administration-sponsored program) to 65 percent (congressionally sponsored program). At the same time, rapid growth in capacity has led to spiraling inflation: 2.8 percent in 1967–68, 7.5 percent a year in 1968–70, and 15 percent in 1970–71. In view of this, even the administration schedule seems excessive. The CEQ expenditure estimate of $38.8 billion seems more attainable, although it is still slightly higher than warranted by the most reasonable expectations of capacity increase. Some initial substitution of investment in collection systems instead of treatment plants would spread the construction over a larger number of firms, permitting a higher level of spending while not straining capacity.[7] The federal share of this $38.8 billion is put at $25.8 billion, which includes existing grant programs of HUD and other agencies as well as the new EPA program.

In this study, then, $38.8 billion will be taken as the total state and local capital investment in water pollution abatement for 1972–80. The average annual rate of investment for the nine years would thus be $4.3 billion whereas from 1965 to 1973 it averaged $2 billion a year. The rate of investment has thus been climbing and can be expected to peak at $5 billion a year by 1977. This rate trend can be considered a minimum, sufficient only to meet expected water quality standards.

URBAN MASS TRANSIT. Traffic congestion, gasoline shortages and price increases, and environmental legislation have aroused public interest in developing more efficient urban mass transit systems. Such programs, whether for buses or rapid rail systems, would necessitate large capital investments. The Urban Mass Transportation Assistance Act of 1970

7. Current plans show an intention to concentrate initially on treatment plants, with upgrading of collection systems later. Concurrent development would reduce capacity strain in any one segment.

provided for the continuation of a grant program (initiated by the Urban Mass Transportation Act of 1964) to assist public agencies in constructing facilities and purchasing equipment for use in public transportation service in urban areas. In light of recent events, the federal government will undoubtedly continue to provide assistance, although the levels of funding and the resultant burden on local budgets remain unclear.

During 1965–72, $2.9 billion worth of projects eligible for capital investment had received federal grant commitments of $1.8 billion. These grant commitments have increased dramatically in recent years, to nearly $1 billion a year in fiscal years 1973 and 1974 from $0.2 billion in fiscal 1970. Fiscal 1975 commitments are estimated at $1.4 billion.[8] These funds are allocated so as to cover two-thirds of nonrecoupable costs. Revenues are typically projected to match operating costs, so nonrecoupable costs are essentially all capital costs. A $1 billion federal share implies an annual financing burden for urban governments of $0.5 billion for mass transit capital facilities.

The average size of capital grants between 1965 and 1972 was about $6.1 million. There have been a few large grants for the construction or expansion of rapid rail systems: $231.2 million for nine projects in the San Francisco BART (Bay Area Rapid Transit) system, $199.9 million for eleven Boston MBTA (Massachusetts Bay Transit Authority) projects, $152.8 million for the New York City Transit Authority.[9] Most grants, however, have been for the purchase of buses and related equipment. There are only ten major rapid rail systems in operation in the United States, with one more, Washington's Metro, still under construction. In view of the small number of existing systems and the long lead time required for construction, it appears that the greatest short-term expansion possibilities are for bus lines.

Buses are less "lumpy" than rapid rail systems and therefore present a simpler allocative problem. Buses come in many sizes, can be ordered in quantities as small as one, require no new rights of way for operation, and need only a short lead time. Although the present grant system favors projects with a high ratio of capital costs to operating costs, and hence rapid rail systems over buses, the President signed a bill (Public Law

8. *The Budget of the United States Government, Fiscal Year 1975—Appendix*, p. 713, and *Fiscal Year 1972*, p. 760.

9. U.S. Department of Transportation, Urban Mass Transportation Administration, *Approvals of Capital Grants and Loans* (1973).

93-503) at the end of 1974 authorizing $11 billion in capital grants to be used instead for operating costs for the next ten years. A shift in emphasis to developing bus systems, perhaps with the construction of express bus lanes on major arteries, may be expected.[10]

The Department of Transportation conducted a survey of capital investment needs and future programs as reported by the states, their subdivisions, and the private sector. The results, described in the 1972 National Transportation Report, gave $63.5 billion (in 1969 dollars) as the upper cost limit of candidate public transportation projects from 1970 to 1990 (see table 2-6). Estimates were also made of possible capital improvement programs based on varying assumptions. The low-funding alternative, not shown in the table, assumes a continuation of categorical grants but with federal funding of only one-half present levels. It is unlikely that urban mass transit would be cut back this much.

Continuing categorical grants and maintaining current federal support give the capital investment program shown in the table as "current federal funding." Transportation expenditures would increase substantially, especially for urban transit, were the federal government to initiate a single grant program, as the administration has proposed. Such a plan would permit funding of any mode of transportation from the same funds with uniform matching requirements. This is the "proposed federal funding" option.

From the table it can be seen that the growth in the public transit sector will continue through the second third of the decade even if the current federal program is not changed. Federal expenditures would increase, of course, under either program. With matching grants of 2 to 1, a peak annual rate of $2.0 billion would mean an urban share of almost $0.7 billion, and the $2.4 billion annual rate of the flexible-funding alternative would mean $0.8 billion these higher spending levels would raise the local share from its 1972–73 level of about $0.5 billion. Thus to meet the capital costs of these programs, the contributions of the urban governments would have to grow at about 20 percent a year for the next two or three years and then stabilize. Although the required increases are large in percentage terms, they take place over a fairly long period and are not excessive in absolute terms.

10. A more detailed discussion of the financing issues can be found in Edward R. Fried, Alice M. Rivlin, Charles L. Schultze, and Nancy H. Teeters, *Setting National Priorities: The 1974 Budget* (Brookings Institution, 1973), pp. 238–52.

Table 2-6. *Estimated Cost of Needed Urban Public Transportation Capital Improvement Programs, Funds Available, and Urban Share, Various Periods, 1970–90*

Description	Billions of 1969 dollars	Billions of 1973 dollars[a]
Cost of needed programs		
Total, 1970–90	63.5	71.4
Annual rate, 1974–90	...	3.4
Funds available, current federal funding program		
Total, 1974–90[b]	27.4	30.8
Annual rate		
1972–73	...	1.5
1974–78	...	2.1
1979–90	...	1.7
Funds available, proposed federal funding program		
Total, 1974–90[c]	31.4	35.3
Annual rate		
1974–78	...	2.4
1979–90	...	2.0
Urban share[d]		
Annual rate		
1972–73	...	0.5
1974–78	...	0.7–0.8
1979–90	...	0.6–0.7

Sources: U.S. Department of Transportation, *1972 National Transportation Report: Present Status—Future Alternatives* (1972), p. xi.

a. Computed from published 1969-dollar values using the implicit price deflator for producers' durable equipment (ratio 1973:1969 = 1.125).

b. Amount available if the level of federal grants in the early 1970s is maintained.

c. Amount available if federal program should be changed, as proposed, to permit funding of all modes of transportation, with uniform matching requirements.

d. Assumes federal funding of two-thirds of the cost.

The Private Sector

Environmental concerns have been most vexing, perhaps, to private industry. Faced with long lead times in production planning and large fixed capital stocks, this sector is now being asked to contend with uncertain future pollution requirements and the equally difficult problem of securing supplies of energy. The ambiguity of the present situation is compounded by unpredictable price levels even when requirements are known. Future production costs seem certain, however, to be boosted by the incorporation of effluent controls that do not increase output. Energy costs relative to output may also be expected to increase because of both pollution abatement devices and the growing scarcity of cheap fuel sources.

As this analysis is confined to the incremental capital costs of social improvement plans, we address only two areas: investment in air and water pollution control by industry, and increased capital expenditures by the energy production sector (fuel suppliers and intermediate processors such as the electric utilities). Although the estimates presented reflect the best knowledge now available, the current state of flux in environmental legislation and the uncertainties of energy supply suggest that these data should be examined primarily for their indications of deviation from current trends rather than as actual spending projections.

POLLUTION ABATEMENT. Expenditures on air and water pollution controls by industry have increased sharply since the late 1960s and will undoubtedly continue to rise as equipment is made to conform to effluent restrictions. The most extensive information on outlays by private industry is provided by the McGraw-Hill annual surveys on pollution control investment spending. The Council on Environmental Quality has incorporated the McGraw-Hill survey data into its estimating procedures, although the CEQ's estimates are much lower. The council reported that the McGraw-Hill expenditures may be overstated through the inclusion of spending that is not directly related to pollution control. When a new plant is built that incorporates a low-pollution process, it is especially difficult to ascertain the fraction of investment directly attributable to pollution control.

The three major components of the private sector's pollution problem are air pollution from stationary sources,[11] water pollution by manufacturing firms, and water pollution by utilities. The CEQ projected total private expenditures for pollution abatement at $33.2 billion, or $3.3 billion a year, for fiscal 1972–81:[12]

	Billions of 1973 dollars
Air pollution, stationary sources	11.7
Water pollution, manufacturing	12.7
Water pollution, utilities	7.0
Other (aircraft, solid waste, etc.)	1.8
Total	33.2

11. Expenditures for pollution control devices in automobiles are excluded from this analysis as the consumer has the option of paying the added cost or substituting a somewhat less expensive vehicle to maintain the same total price. Moreover, these devices on mobile sources are not factors in the industrial capital-output relationship.

12. Derived from *Environmental Quality, The Fourth Annual Report of the Council on Environmental Quality,* p. 93.

The McGraw-Hill estimates, although they are not directly comparable because of the different times covered, are notably higher:[13]

	Billions of current dollars		
	1972	1973	1976
Air pollution	2.8	3.6	4.1
Water pollution	1.7	2.6	3.0
Total	4.5	6.2	7.1

Some businesses, because of the nature of their production processes, face much higher pollution control costs than others. Among durable goods industries, metal, stone, clay, and glass manufacturers reported planned investment in pollution abatement at levels substantially higher than in the past. The paper, chemicals, and petroleum industries are responsible for the large shares of capital to be devoted to pollution control by nondurable goods manufacturers. In 1973 the paper industry planned to spend nearly half of its total investment funds on pollution control. Electric utilities will be spending proportionately less on pollution control during the remainder of the decade, although the sheer size of the industry will account for its spending more than any other:[14]

	Expenditures as a percentage of capital spending		
	1972	1973	1976
Durable manufacturing	6.6	8.3	8.4
Nondurable manufacturing	9.8	12.2	13.8
Electric utilities	7.9	6.8	5.9
All business	5.1	5.9	5.9

The higher McGraw-Hill estimates have been incorporated in the private sector claims discussed later in this chapter.

ENERGY PRODUCTION. The energy crisis focused attention on the capital financing needs of the domestic energy industry. In this section some projections of U.S. energy demand and supply are outlined and used as a basis for estimating the capital requirements of the industry through 1980.

A study by the National Petroleum Council projected the energy demand-supply balance to 1985 for alternative assumptions about de-

13. McGraw-Hill, "Sixth Annual Survey of Pollution Control Expenditures" (McGraw-Hill, 1973; processed).
14. Ibid.

mand growth and supply.[15] The NPC's intermediate case III is shown in table 2-7. Energy consumption is projected to grow at 4.2 percent a year —in line with historical trends and potential GNP growth. (This basic projection assumes no change in the real price of energy.)

To meet this demand, the NPC predicts a sharp rise in domestic oil and gas exploration, expansion of nuclear power supplies at the most favorable forecast rate of the Atomic Energy Commission, and an acceleration of domestic coal production. However, "finding rates" per foot drilled for oil and gas are assumed to remain at present low rates, and supplies of synthetic gas are not significant before 1980. As a result, energy imports continue to rise sharply during the 1970s at a 12.1 percent annual rate. Imports reach 26 percent of total consumption in 1980, more than twice the 12 percent of 1970.

The NPC study also provides (chapter 14) cumulative fifteen-year estimates of the capital required for its supply projections: $501 billion (in 1970 dollars) for 1971–85, excluding marketing and distribution costs. Table 2-8 shows an estimated annual pattern of capital outlays for the 1970s that is consistent with the cumulative estimates. Investment expenditures rise at an annual rate well above that of the previous decade, an average annual growth of 8.1 percent in real terms as against 4.3 percent. The largest dollar amounts are in electric utilities with much of the growth resulting from the more capital-intensive nuclear fuel plants. However, the growth of utility investment is not much greater than that of the 1960s, even though it is above other projections for the industry.[16]

The most significant growth of capital outlays is in oil and natural gas. Adjusted for inflation, domestic investment in this sector grew at very modest rates in the 1960s; it would have to increase greatly to hold imported energy needs to the levels shown in table 2-7. The largest increases are projected for exploration and production, refineries, and the Alaskan pipeline.

If total investment is projected at its 1973 share of GNP, the proportion going to energy investment would rise from 24 percent in 1970 to

15. The council used four sets of assumptions ranging from high demand and supply to a continuation of current trends, which are labeled cases I–IV. See National Petroleum Council, *U.S. Energy Outlook: A Report of the National Petroleum Council's Committee on U.S. Energy Outlook* (1972).

16. For example, see *Electrical World*, vol. 180 (September 15, 1973), p. 53. Utility investment is projected to rise in real terms at 2.8 percent a year between 1973 and 1980.

Table 2-7. *Balance of Energy Supply and Consumption for the United States, Selected Periods, 1960–85*

Source or use	Quadrillions of BTUs a year				Annual growth rate (percent)	
	1970	*1975*	*1980*	*1985*	*1960–70*[a]	*1970–80*
Domestic supply	59.4	64.3	76.2	90.0	3.9	2.5
Oil	21.0	19.8	24.0	25.3	3.3	1.3
Gas	22.4	22.8	21.5	23.1	5.4	−0.4
Hydropower	2.7	3.0	3.2	3.3	4.8	1.7
Geothermal capacity	*	0.1	0.3	0.5	...	...
Coal and nuclear capacity (used)[b]	13.3	18.6	27.1	37.8	2.6	7.4
Coal available	13.1	15.6	18.3	21.4	2.6	3.4
Nuclear power available	0.2	4.0	9.8	20.2	...	...
Imports, to achieve balance	8.4	19.2	26.4	34.9	7.1	12.1
Oil	7.5	18.0	22.5	28.5	6.5	11.8
Gas	1.0	1.2	3.9	6.4	18.1	14.6
Domestic consumption	67.8	83.5	102.6	124.9	4.2	4.2
Fuels used by electric utilities[c]	16.7	23.5	33.0	44.4	7.1	7.1
Oil	2.1	3.5	4.1	4.5	14.0	6.9
Gas	3.9	3.9	3.9	3.9	8.4	0.0
Coal	7.8	8.9	14.3	13.9	5.8	6.3
Nuclear power[d]	0.2	4.3	7.5	18.7	...	...
Hydropower	2.7	3.0	3.2	3.3	4.8	1.7

Sources: National Petroleum Council, *U.S. Energy Outlook: A Report of the National Petroleum Council's Committee on U.S. Energy Outlook* (1972), tables 7, 18, pp. 20, 32 (the projections are the NPC's intermediate case III described in the text); Walter G. Dupree, Jr., and James A. West, *United States Energy through the Year 2000*, Department of the Interior (1972), appendix tables. Figures are rounded.

a. The 1960–70 growth rates, derived from the Interior study, are based on data that are slightly different in some classifications from the NPC study data used for the BTU values.

b. Beginning in 1975, somewhat more coal and nuclear energy is available than is used.

c. Electric utilities are the only consumers of all forms of primary energy; by 1975 this sector is expected to be the largest user of primary fuels in the United States. Thus it is pivotal in developing a balance of energy demand and supply.

d. Includes geothermal energy.

* Less than 0.05.

33 percent in 1980. Not all of these capital outlays would be counted as investment in the national income accounts. The oil and gas estimates, in particular, include leasing payments, exploration costs, and land purchases. However, the projections do provide a rough basis for anticipating high capital requirements for the energy industry.

At present, the announced goal of "independence" makes capital requirements even more uncertain. The target date of 1985 would be extremely costly if independence were interpreted literally. However, the

Table 2-8. *Capital Investment of Energy Industries and of All Industries, Selected Periods, 1960–80*

Billions of 1973 dollars and percent

Description	Capital needed					Annual growth (percent)	
	1960	*1970*	*1973*[a]	*1977*[b]	*1980*[b]	*1960–70*	*1970–80*
Electric utilities	7.3	15.3	19.0	26.5	33.0	7.7	8.0
Oil, natural gas, and synthetics[c]	10.2	11.1	13.5	21.0	24.5	1.9	8.3
Coal and nuclear[d]	0.5	1.0	1.0	1.5	2.0	7.2	7.2
Total energy investment	18.0	27.4	33.5	49.0	59.5	4.3	8.1
Nonresidential investment, all industries	69.1	113.7	136.2	161.0[e]	182.7[e]	5.1	4.9
Energy investment as a percentage of nonresidential investment	26.0	24.1	24.6	30.4	32.6	...	...

Sources: The 1960–73 data are from the following sources.

Electric utilities: Electrical World, vol. 180 (September 15, 1973), p. 53, and earlier issues, adjusted to 1973 prices with the Handy-Whitman construction cost index for electric light and power plants, published in U.S. Bureau of Domestic Commerce, *Construction Review*, vol. 20 (November 1974), p. 52, and earlier issues.

Oil, natural gas, and synthetics: Richard C. Sparling and others, *Capital Investments of the World Petroleum Industry, 1972* (Chase Manhattan Bank, 1973), and preceding issues (chemicals are excluded); American Gas Association, Department of Statistics, *1972 Gas Facts: A Statistical Record of the Gas Utility Industry in 1972* (AGA, 1973), and earlier issues. The data were adjusted to 1973 prices with the nonresidential investment deflator from *Survey of Current Business*, vol. 54 (July 1974), and earlier July issues, and the Handy-Whitman construction cost index for gas plants, published in *Construction Review* (cited above).

Coal and nuclear: Estimated by authors.

Total nonresidential investment: Survey of Current Business (July 1974), and earlier July issues.

The 1971–80 projections are derived from *U.S. Energy Outlook: A Report of the National Petroleum Council's Committee on U.S. Energy Outlook*, chap. 14, by annual interpolation of the NPC's 1971–85 cumulative investment requirements for case III, adjusted to include investment for marketing and distribution.

a. Estimates.

b. Projections.

c. Includes investment in production, refinery, transportation, and marketing facilities.

d. Excludes investment for rail transportation, except 1971–80 projections, where rail is included in the underlying NPC data.

e. The share of gross national product in 1977 and 1980 is assumed to be the same as in 1973.

United States could not obtain real independence by eliminating imports since such an option is not available to its trading allies. Nor is there reason to oppose imports from areas such as Canada and Venezuela as long as these countries do not have a dominant influence. It seems most realistic to interpret the goal as one of increasing alternative energy sources and storage facilities. The first objective has already been given a strong push in the non-Arab countries by the oil price increases.

Even with the goal of "independence," there are several reasons for anticipating increases in domestic energy investment only slightly above those of table 2-8. First, the NPC assumed a change in energy policy in its case III supply projections. Before 1973–74 there was no indication that policy would change in such a way as to make the high exploration projections of case III likely. These projections are close to a maximum feasible rate of expansion and could not be raised significantly within the decade.

Second, the NPC supply projections assumed substantial increases in the real price of energy, but these price increases were not incorporated into the demand estimates—if they had been, reliance on imports would have been reduced. The basic approach to supply was to project quantities and then derive the prices at various assumed rates of return (in 1970 dollars). Imports, controlled through a quota, were used as a balance. In case III, by 1980 the relative prices of primary fuels had increased 200 percent for natural gas, 150 percent for oil, and 30 percent for coal. The impact on the final demand estimates of energy prices of a 100 percent rise in primary prices varied from 25 to 50 percent according to the ultimate use (residential, industrial, transportation, generation of electricity) and averaged about 35 percent.

Future capital requirements of the energy industry are especially difficult to predict because of the dramatic rise in world prices of primary fuels—particularly oil. Current estimates of the price sensitivity of energy demand are bound to be uncertain. Because there have been no sharp price changes in the past our ability to evaluate the implications of this change in the world petroleum market is limited. The NPC study used long-run elasticities of -0.2 for transportation, -0.4 for residential, -0.4 for industrial, and -0.15 for the generation of electricity. If we use the NPC estimates as being in the conservative range and assume an overall rise in real prices of primary fuels by 1975 to 100 percent above those of 1970, the NPC estimates of consumption in 1980 could be reduced by 6 percent and imports held to 20 percent of demand rather than the projected level of 26 percent.

Other studies, begun after the climb of world oil prices in late 1973, have provided estimates of energy demand substantially below those of the National Petroleum Council.[17] The projections are lower principally

17. See, for example, Michael Kennedy, "An Economic Model of the World Oil Market," and Edward A. Hudson and Dale W. Jorgenson, "U.S. Energy Policy and

because the prices of all fuels had increased and higher estimates of the price elasticities of demand were made. For electric utilities these forecasts indicate levels of demand in 1980 as much as 30 percent below the NPC estimates.[18] These projections imply much lower investment requirements for the energy industry. In addition, higher energy prices could be expected to slow the substitution of energy-intensive capital equipment for labor in other sectors of the economy.

A one-time price increase will lower the level of energy demand but not its equilibrium growth rate. Thus it is not a permanent solution. However, price increases are likely to be a major means of maintaining the demand-supply balance until the growth of domestic energy supply is brought into line with that of demand in the 1980s.

Finally, many of the proposed near-term increases in supply are in the least capital-intensive areas, such as coal and secondary oil recovery. A switch to greater use of coal also implies some saving in refinery capacity for imported oil. Currently, it seems reasonable to view case III as a high projection of post–"oil crisis" capital needs.

Government Budgets

The budget projections for the federal government and for state and local governments in tables 2-9 and 2-10 show only the future costs of present program commitments and the funds that would become available under the present tax structure. They are not forecasts of actual expenditures or revenues since they make no allowance for new programs or the cancellation of existing ones.[19] In addition, they are based on the assumed full employment growth path outlined at the beginning of this chapter.

Economic Growth, 1975–2000," both in Bell Journal of Economics and Management Science, vol. 5 (Autumn 1974), pp. 540–77 and 461–514 respectively; T. D. Mount and L. D. Chapman, "Electricity Demand Projections and Utility Capital Requirements," Cornell Agricultural Economics Staff Paper (Cornell University, September 1974; processed).

18. Mount and Chapman, "Electricity Demand Projections," p. 12.

19. This section relies heavily on a previously published study of the 1975 budget. Except for a higher assumed rate of inflation and the interim path of unemployment, the estimates are consistent with those contained in Barry M. Blechman, Edward M. Gramlich, and Robert W. Hartman, *Setting National Priorities: The 1975 Budget* (Brookings Institution, 1974).

Table 2-9. *Receipts and Expenditures of the Federal Government,*
National Income Accounts Basis, Selected Periods,
Calendar Years 1960–80

Billions of current dollars and percent

Description	Actual			Projected		Average annual change (percent)		
	1960	1970	1973	1977	1980	1960–70	1970–73	1973–80
Receipts	96.5	192.0	265.3	416.6	554.2	7.1	11.4	11.1
Personal taxes and nontaxes	43.6	92.2	114.5	201.8	284.8	7.8	7.5	13.9
Corporate profits tax accruals	21.7	31.0	49.7	69.2	87.5	3.6	17.0	8.4
Indirect business taxes	13.5	19.3	21.0	27.5	30.9	3.6	2.9	5.7
Contributions for social insurance	17.7	49.5	80.1	118.1	151.0	10.8	17.4	9.5
Expenditures	93.0	203.9	264.0	385.9	472.4	8.1	9.0	8.7
Purchases of goods and services	53.5	96.2	106.6	151.4	190.5	6.0	3.5	8.7
Transfer payments	23.4	63.2	95.5	155.4	196.5	10.5	14.8	10.9
Grants-in-aid	6.5	24.4	40.9	56.1	62.4	14.1	18.8	6.2
Net interest	7.1	14.6	15.9	20.0	20.0	7.5	2.9	3.3
Subsidies *less* current surplus of government enterprises	2.5	5.5	5.1	3.0	3.0	8.2	−2.5	−7.3
Surplus or deficit	3.5	−11.9	1.3	30.7	81.8	...	...	...

Sources: *Survey of Current Business,* February 1974, and earlier issues; and authors' projections. Figures are rounded.

Thus they do not reflect cyclical influences on expenditure or revenue in any specific year.

The Federal Government

Federal revenues are projected to rise 11.1 percent annually between 1973 and 1980. This high growth rate—substantially above that of money GNP—is due to the progressive nature of the personal income tax system. Rising income, whether from inflation or real growth, moves people into higher tax brackets and thus raises the average tax rate as well as the base to which it is applied. These revenue projections incorporate an income elasticity of 1.5 for the personal income tax. This is higher than the estimate used in making many previous projections as well as the projections of the annual budget document, but is supported by several recent studies.[20] This implicit tax rate increase will amount to about $65 billion by 1980 (based on the fiscal 1974 tax rate structure).

20. For example, see Joseph A. Pechman, "Responsiveness of the Federal Individual Income Tax to Changes in Income," *Brookings Papers on Economic Activity* (2:1973), pp. 390–94.

Until recently, the effect on total revenues of the progressive personal income tax was partially offset by the low income elasticity of the social security tax. However, the social security system has been reformed and provides for automatic increases in the taxable earnings ceiling as incomes rise instead of requiring legislative action. In the future, taxes other than the personal income tax will rise almost proportionately to the increases in nominal GNP.

Expenditures are projected to rise less than revenues. Much of the 8.7 percent annual growth results from raising current program costs to cover pay and price increases. But expenditures also rise significantly in real terms, mostly because of spending for defense and the income security programs. The defense increases can be attributed to the future costs of the current defense program.[21] Force reductions in Southeast Asia cease to offset increases in other areas. A stepped-up rate of weapon modernization and new undertakings by the strategic forces are responsible for most of the increases. The growth in defense outlays between 1975 and 1980 is estimated at $21 billion.[22]

Substantial increases are also projected for the income security programs. Even if prices remained constant, the total for social security benefits would have to be increased to take care of a growing number of beneficiaries, many of whom, as new retirees, have a higher income base than those who became eligible earlier. In addition, benefit increases are now tied to increases in the cost of living. Several other programs, such as supplemental security income and food stamps, will experience a rapid influx of new recipients. Increases in grant programs above 1975 levels are limited principally to Environmental Protection Agency grants for the construction of waste treatment plants and grants to cover the growing numbers of beneficiaries of the health care and income maintenance programs. General revenue sharing is assumed to continue beyond 1977 at previous real per capita levels.

The combination of revenue and expenditure projections results in a large rise in the "fiscal dividend," to $82 billion by 1980, which is a budget

---

21. The projected defense expenditures are discussed more fully in Blechman and others, *Setting National Priorities,* chapter 4, and are summarized in table 4-10 of that study. Their underlying philosophy is somewhat different from that of the projections for other programs since they are based on the currently defined defense posture rather than legislation and can be changed by decisions of Congress in future years.

22. Ibid., pp. 250–53.

indicator of the funds available for new programs and tax reductions.[23] Our estimates of the budget surplus are substantially above those of the 1975 budget document, a difference primarily attributable to the higher rate of inflation assumed for the rest of the decade. The methods used to project expenditures imply that they will rise about 1 percent in the long run for each 1 percent increase in price levels. However, because of the progressive structure of the personal income tax, total revenues would rise about 1.2 percent. In addition, 1980 revenues would rise by about $20 billion as a result of the drop to a 4 percent unemployment rate from the 4.9 percent of 1973. On the expenditure side, these projections incorporate a much higher future cost estimate of current defense programs than the long-term projections of the 1975 budget document.

State and Local Governments

For more than a decade state and local governments have been the most rapidly expanding sector of the economy. In the 1960s these governments' purchases of goods and services rose at an annual rate of 10.3 percent whereas the annual rate for the whole economy was 6.9 percent. Much of this greater than average growth of expenditures can be traced to the high labor-intensiveness of state and local purchases. Without the offsetting influence of increasing labor productivity, the prices these governments pay rise more rapidly than prices in the general economy. In constant dollars, their purchases grew at a 5.4 percent rate as against 4 percent for constant-dollar GNP. The costs of educating the children born in the postwar "baby boom" and the increasing demand for public services were significant sources of the growth. Although welfare programs were partially financed by the federal government, expenditures on health care and welfare rose at an annual rate of 15.5 percent in the last half of the decade.

This rapid increase in expenditures placed extreme pressure on the financial position of state and local governments. Particularly for local governments, dependent on the property tax, the accelerating inflation raised expenditures faster than revenues. To make up the difference, these governments levied new taxes and raised existing tax rates. However,

23. This is a budget concept only and does not necessarily indicate actual resource availability in future years. The latter will depend on the strength of private demand and public needs relative to potential output.

Table 2-10. *Receipts and Expenditures of State and Local Governments, National Income Accounts Basis, Selected Periods, Calendar Years 1960–80*

Billions of current dollars and percent

Description	Actual			Projected		Average annual rate of growth		
	1960	1970	1973	1977	1980	1960–70	1970–73	1973–80
Receipts	49.9	135.0	194.5	290.9	363.1	10.5	12.9	9.3
Personal taxes and nontaxes	7.3	24.4	38.4	65.9	90.3	12.8	16.3	13.0
Corporate profits tax accruals	1.3	3.8	6.4	8.8	11.6	11.3	19.0	8.9
Indirect business taxes	31.8	74.1	96.8	139.5	171.6	8.8	9.3	8.5
Contributions for social insurance	3.0	8.3	12.0	20.6	27.2	10.7	13.1	12.4
Federal grants-in-aid	6.5	24.4	40.9	56.1	62.4	14.1	18.8	6.2
Expenditures	49.6	133.2	184.0	289.6	381.2	10.4	11.4	11.0
Purchases of goods and services	46.1	123.3	170.5	273.0	356.8	10.3	11.4	11.1
Compensation for services	25.6	69.6	94.8	149.2	199.8	10.5	10.9	11.2
Buildings	12.4	25.1	28.3	45.2	54.5	7.0	4.1	9.8
Other	8.1	28.7	47.3	78.6	102.5	13.5	18.1	11.7
Transfer payments	5.1	14.1	19.5	23.8	32.2	10.7	11.4	7.4
Net interest	0.7	−0.4	−1.3	−1.6	−1.6	...	...	...
Subsidies *less* current surplus of government enterprises	−2.2	−3.8	−4.7	−5.6	−6.2	...	...	...
Surplus or deficit	0.3	1.8	10.5	1.3	−18.1	...	...	...

Sources: *Survey of Current Business*, March 1974, and earlier issues; and authors' projections. Figures are rounded.

much of the gap was closed by federal grants-in-aid, which increased at an annual rate of 17 percent during the 1965–70 period. Revenue sharing contributed to an even higher 19 percent growth in the first three years of the 1970s.

The revenue projections of table 2-10 are based on an assumption of constant tax rates. The elasticities of individual taxes with respect to GNP range from 1.7 for personal income taxes to 0.5 for various excise taxes.[24] Under these assumptions, revenues will grow at an annual rate of 9.3 percent—which is proportionate to GNP—between 1973 and 1980. The slowing of the rate of growth results from holding federal grants in aid to current commitments—the increase of grants is far below that of the previous eight years. This reflects the federal government's assumption of direct responsibility, through transfer payments, for income support payments to the elderly and disabled; a projected lower growth in beneficiaries of Aid to Families with Dependent Children; and an expenditure ceiling

24. The estimated tax elasticities are taken from Tax Foundation, Inc., *The Financial Outlook for State and Local Governments to 1980* (New York: Tax Foundation, 1973), p. 88.

on grants for social services. Also, these baseline projections make no allowance for increasing tax rates.

Some moderation of the growth in state and local expenditures in real terms is projected for the last half of the decade,[25] although inflation will continue to generate high growth rates in nominal terms. Employment growth should slow with the end of the boom in school enrollment. Capital outlays, as discussed earlier, should show major increases in real terms only for the construction of waste treatment plants and mass transit. These increases will be partially offset by less school construction and completion of the major portion of the interstate highway program. Total construction outlays are projected to rise at a 9.8 percent rate between 1973 and 1980, somewhat higher than the annual average of 7.0 percent in the 1960s.

Payments to vendors of medical services and other expenditures (primarily on welfare programs and capital outlays for equipment) will continue to grow rapidly, but the projected increases are well below those of the recent past. Employee retirement and income support payments cause most of the growth in transfers.

Since the projected growth of expenditures exceeds the rise in revenue generated by constant tax rates and the assumed low increase in grants, the aggregate state and local government budget gradually shifts to a deficit of $18 billion by 1980. However, this deficit is far smaller than in the previous decade. The high 1973 surplus is dominated by the sudden infusion of general revenue sharing funds and the rapid rise of revenues following the 1970 recession.

The fiscal outlook for most state and local governments has improved considerably over that for the 1960s. In real terms expenditure growth is moderating, and the increased emphasis on income taxes makes it easier to adjust to inflation without resorting to tax rate increases. The fiscal problem will continue to be severe in specific areas such as the large metropolitan centers, but the overall pressure will ease.

---

25. The expenditure projections include allowances for pay and price increases, larger numbers of program beneficiaries, and historical rates of growth in real outlays per beneficiary. Although the estimates are constructed within the framework of the national income accounts rather than that of the Bureau of the Census, they are derived primarily from Tax Foundation, *The Financial Outlook for State and Local Governments to 1980*. Exceptions are separate treatment of capital outlays and employment costs and, for programs to which federal grants are particularly important, underlying assumptions that are consistent with the federal budget projections.

Private Claims on Resources

For a true picture of the claims on total resources, it is necessary to make projections for the remaining components of private demand. These are personal consumption expenditures, business investment other than for energy sources and pollution abatement, net exports, and inventory accumulation. For these we relied heavily on long-term projections made by the National Planning Association and the Bureau of Labor Statistics.[26]

Personal Consumption Expenditures

Although the saving rate has always been viewed as stable, in the last half of the 1960s it became quite volatile. This is only partly explainable by cyclical changes in income, unemployment, and the rate of inflation. The uncertainties of forecasting future trends in the saving rate are evident in the wide disparity between the estimates of the NPA and the BLS—5.5 and 6.9 percent respectively in 1980—a difference representing over $20 billion at 1973 prices. In the absence of any clear indications of future trends, we have held the ratio of consumption to disposable income at the 1972–73 level. This means a slight fall in the saving rate from 6.2 in 1973 to 5.6 because consumer interest payments continue to rise faster than income. Taxable personal income (excluding transfer payments but including personal social insurance taxes) was projected as a constant share of GNP. The growth of consumption expenditures is thus less than that of GNP because of the rising average tax rate embodied in the baseline federal revenue projections.

Business Investment

Business investment is projected to rise faster than GNP because of the large increases in investment of the energy industry. We have extrapolated the ratio of investment (excluding pollution abatement and energy) to real private output at a constant but historically high level of 9.25.[27] This

---

26. Graham C. Scott, *U.S. Economic and Demographic Projections, 1972–81,* National Economic Projection Series 72-N-2 (National Planning Association, 1973); and Kutscher, "Projections of GNP, Income, Output, and Employment."

27. This is consistent with the implications of the investment equations of several large econometric models used for forecasting and those of the Federal Reserve Board and Data Resources, Inc.

Table 2-11. *Gross National Product in Constant Dollars, by Major Component, Selected Years, 1960–80*

Billions of 1973 dollars

Component	Actual			Projected		Percentage distribution		
	1960	1970	1973	1977	1980	1960	1973	1980
Gross national product	758.0	1,118.4	1,289.1	1,524.7	1,730.2	100.0	100.0	100.0
Personal consumption expenditures	458.4	693.6	804.0	942.7	1,058.9	60.5	62.4	61.2
Nonresidential investment	74.0	119.3	144.2	188.4	215.6	9.8	11.2	12.5
Fixed	69.1	113.7	136.2	172.0	199.9	9.1	10.6	11.6
Inventory accumulation	4.9	5.6	8.0	16.4	15.7	0.6	0.6	0.9
Residential construction	37.3	37.9	58.0	57.3	56.3	4.9	4.5	3.3
Net exports	4.9	0.1	5.8	6.5	9.7	0.6	0.4	0.6
Federal government purchases	97.0	120.5	106.6	117.4	129.6	12.8	8.3	7.5
State and local government purchases	86.4	146.7	170.5	206.4	231.8	11.4	13.2	13.4
Unallocated resources	0	0	0	6.2	28.3	...	...	1.6

Sources: *Survey of Current Business*, February 1974, and earlier issues; and authors' projections. Figures are rounded.

is based on the assumption that strong investment demand for the industries producing basic materials, where capacity utilization has been high in recent years, will be partially offset by lower capacity growth in the finished goods industries. Fixed investment outlays for the energy industry were assumed to follow the pattern shown in table 2-8. Pollution abatement outlays were projected at the 1973 ratio to total investment indicated in the McGraw-Hill surveys.

Total Claims on Resources

The distribution of the total claims on resources is shown in tables 2-11 and 2-12.

If the projected capital needs of the energy sector were to be met, business investment (in 1973 dollars) would grow from 11.2 percent of GNP in 1973 to 12.5 percent by 1980. This would be offset in part by a declining share of output for residential construction. Government purchases exclusive of new programs would increase slightly less than GNP. The rising average personal tax rate is reflected in a low assumed growth of disposable income, and thus a declining share of GNP going to personal consumption expenditures. This would make a small surplus of $28.3 billion (in 1973 dollars) available by 1980.

Table 2-12. *Gross National Product in Current Dollars, by Major Component, Selected Years, 1960–80*

Billions of current dollars

Component	Actual			Projected	
	1960	1970	1973	1977	1980
Gross national product	503.7	977.1	1,289.1	1,896.8	2,387.5
Personal consumption expenditures	325.2	617.6	804.0	1,158.4	1,424.8
Nonresidential investment	52.0	105.1	144.2	229.2	287.5
Fixed	48.4	100.6	136.2	211.2	269.5
Inventory accumulation	3.6	4.5	8.0	18.0	18.0
Residential construction	22.8	31.2	58.0	75.8	83.5
Net exports	4.0	3.6	5.8	2.5	1.1
Federal government purchases	53.5	96.2	106.6	151.4	190.5
State and local government purchases	46.1	123.4	170.5	273.0	356.8
Unallocated resources	0	0	0	6.5	43.5

Sources: *Survey of Current Business*, February 1974, and earlier issues; and authors' projections. Figures are rounded.

Some Implications of the Projections

Projections such as the foregoing are frequently used to examine the potential resources available for new programs in the federal budget. If examined solely from the budget side, the 1980 surplus of $82 billion (table 2-9) implies that considerable revenues would be available for tax reduction or new expenditure. This follows from an assumption that the appropriate budget balance at full employment is zero. But the uncommitted resources of $43.5 billion (table 2-12) are far lower than the budget surplus. If the surplus were used for increased government expenditures or reductions in the personal income tax (and this increased personal consumption), total claims on resources would exceed the supply. This is because we have projected a high level of business investment and assumed that there would be no change in tax rates. Thus the surplus is due to a high estimate of revenue growth rather than a low estimate of expenditure growth. On the other hand, state and local government revenue growth, with fixed tax rates, is not adequate to finance their increased expenditures; and the investment needs of businesses exceed their cash flow of retained earnings and capital consumption. As a result, a substantial portion of the budget surplus has already been used up in the projections as income transfers through the capital markets to other sectors.

The relation between the budget surplus and uncommitted resources is shown by the projected pattern of saving and investment in table 2-13.[28] As in the past, the household sector would be a net supplier of funds to the capital markets. In addition to personal savings, purchase of homes (mainly single-family houses) and capital consumption allowances on homes have been allocated to the household sector. Following conventions of the flow-of-funds accounts, we have also included the retirement credits of state and local government trust funds. Growth in personal saving is held down in the projection period by the rising average tax rate on personal income, but this is offset by a lower rate of increase in home purchases. As a percentage of GNP, net household saving is the same in 1980 as in 1973.

The business sector has a substantial deficit as funds from internal sources fall short of investment needs. However, the sharp rise in energy investment is partially offset by an increase (attributable to high prices) in the earnings retained by the fuel industries. In 1980 the net external funds requirement as a percentage of GNP is only slightly larger than in 1973.

The major change in the surplus-deficit position is in the government sector. Under the assumption of constant tax rates the rise in the federal surplus is offset by a growing deficit for state and local governments. The general fund position of these governments is emphasized in table 2-14 by removing the debt retirement fund surplus. Such a deficit could not actually occur since, by law, many of these governments cannot engage in deficit financing. Normally state and local governments can be expected to finance a substantial proportion of capital outlays in the bond markets, but they do not borrow to finance current account deficits. Estimates described in the next chapter indicate that state and local governments can be expected to borrow at the rate of about $33 billion for capital projects in 1980. However, this gross borrowing would be offset by debt retirement of $14.5 billion (see table 2-14). Also, state and local governments can be expected to accumulate financial assets of $10.5 billion a year. Net borrowing (deficit) would thus amount to only about $8 billion. If the expenditure needs are to be met, the gap of $25 billion would be fi-

---

28. Although the table presents estimates based on unemployment rates of 4 percent and 5 percent, the figures in this discussion are at the 4 percent rate.

Table 2-13. *Saving and Investment, by Major Sector, 1960, 1973, and 1980*

Billions of dollars

Description	1960	1973	1980	
			4 percent unemployment	*5 percent unemployment*
Household sector, net saving	**4.8**	**33.5**	**60.4**	**58.9**
Saving				
Personal	17.0	54.8	88.0	86.5
Retirement credits of state and local government trust funds[a]	2.2	8.4	15.0	15.0
Capital consumption allowances[b]	5.3	10.4	13.4	13.4
Investment				
Residential home purchases[b]	19.7	40.1	56.0	56.0
Business sector, net saving	**−3.6**	**−37.4**	**−71.3**	**−70.3**
Saving				
Retained earnings	13.2	42.7	71.9	68.2
Inventory valuation adjustment	0.2	−17.3	−4.5	−4.5
Capital consumption allowances[b]	38.1	99.2	176.3	175.0
Gross domestic investment[b]	55.1	162.0	315.0	309.0
Government sector, net saving	**1.6**	**3.3**	**5.2**	**10.7**
Federal surplus[c]	3.5	1.2	13.2	18.7
State and local government surplus	−1.9	2.1	−8.0	−8.0
Net foreign investment	**1.7**	**2.2**	**−3.1**	**1.9**
Statistical discrepancy	**−1.0**	**2.9**	**2.5**	**2.5**
Addenda				
Total unallocated resources[e]	0	0	13.5	19.0
Federal full employment surplus	...	...	13.2	31.7[d]

Sources: *Survey of Current Business*, February 1974, and earlier issues; Board of Governors of the Federal Reserve System, "Flow of Funds Accounts, 1945–72" (1973; processed), and "Flow of Funds, Unadjusted, 4th Quarter, 1973, Preliminary" (February 8, 1974; processed); and authors' projections. Figures are rounded.

a. The national income accounts surplus of state and local governments is adjusted to exclude retirement funds, which are shifted to the household sector in this table.

b. Residential home purchase and capital consumption on homes, included in the business sector in the national income accounts, have been shifted to the household sector here.

c. The federal surplus in 1980 is adjusted to include unallocated resources and the financing gap of state and local governments from table 2-14 as expenditures.

d. The full employment surplus in 1980 differs from the actual surplus of the 5 percent unemployment case because it is calculated on the traditional basis of revenues associated with a 4 percent unemployment rate.

Table 2-14. *Derivation of State and Local Government Financing Gap,*
1980[a]

Billions of dollars

	Unemployment rate	
Description	4 percent	5 percent
Initial deficit	18.1[b]	24.1
Less pension fund credits	15.0	15.0
Total government deficit	33.1	39.1
Net borrowing[c]	8.0	8.0
Financing gap[d]	25.1	31.1

Source: Derived by authors.
a. Assumes constant tax rates.
b. From table 2-10.
c. Net borrowing equals gross bond financing of $33 billion minus debt retirement of $14.5 billion minus accumulation of financial assets of $10.5 billion.
d. The gap is equal to the general government deficit minus net borrowing. This is the amount of funds that must be offset by expenditure reductions, tax rate increases, or increased federal grants. We have assumed a matching increase in federal grants.

nanced by legislated tax increases, higher federal grants-in-aid, or federal assumption of some state and local programs. The latter two methods would reduce the federal surplus without changing the amount of uncommitted resources. For example, if grants to state and local governments in relation to their expenditures were maintained at the 1973 level, the federal contribution would be increased by $22 billion. This would leave only $3 billion to be raised by tax increases. Thus revenue raised by tax increases would be less than 2 percent of the total increase in state and local revenue between 1973 and 1980, whereas between 1965 and 1970 these governments had to raise over one-third of their revenue through legislated tax increases.[29]

Our projections deviate from historical patterns in holding future grants to the level required by current programs and in assuming constant tax rates. In the past, a substantial portion of the potential federal surplus was transferred to state and local governments through grants-in-aid and tax rate reductions that partially offset local increases. A similar process will probably continue. Since we wish to focus on the implications for fiscal policy, we have offset the state and local government financing gap of $25.1 billion with federal grants. In addition, the unallocated resources

29. Tax Foundation, *The Financial Outlook for State and Local Governments to 1980*, p. 86.

of $43.5 billion were assigned to federal purchases. This reduces the federal budget surplus from $81.8 billion to $13.2 billion.[30]

The projections do not imply a dramatic change in the provision of resources for business investment. In part, the declining share of residential construction offsets the increased investment in energy and raw materials. The slower growth of finished goods industries also yields some capital savings. On the financing side, there is an increase from 1973 levels in the share of GNP going to profits plus inventory valuation adjustment. This share climbs from 8.5 percent in 1973 to 9.4 percent in 1980. Primarily, it is a cyclical factor and shows a return to a higher rate of resource utilization together with higher rates of return in the fuel and raw material industries. It is below the 1965–66 peak of 11 percent.

Since 1966 corporate profits as a percentage of GNP have dropped substantially. This change cannot be fully explained by cyclical factors. In part, it is due to more liberal tax laws, which have shifted a portion of taxable profits to capital consumption allowances. There have also been changes in the factors determining the profit rate that will provide an adequate level of investment, such as the cost-of-funds and risk premiums.[31] Any projection of the future share of profits is uncertain, and one must therefore be cautious about concluding that there will be no serious financing problem. Taxable profits as a share of GNP rise only slightly in the projections because the assumed moderation of inflation reduces the capital gain on inventories from its present high level.

A continuation of the current inflation implies an increase in the tax rate on business income. This is similar to the previously discussed increase in the average rate paid under the personal income tax. Because capital consumption allowances are based on historical capital costs rather than replacement costs, they do not expand proportionately with GNP during periods of accelerating inflation. Hence, a growing fraction of total

30. In table 2-13 the $43.5 billion in unallocated resources are assumed to raise federal expenditures. This is done to simplify the presentation. The use of the unallocated resources for private consumption (that is, a tax cut) would result in a larger figure for household saving, since some of the increased income would not be spent, and thus a smaller required federal surplus. There would be an even larger reduction of the required federal surplus if the tax reduction were directed toward business. This reflects a general belief that the propensity of business to spend additional income is less than that of households.

31. A recent detailed analysis of the profit share and the issues involved is found in William D. Nordhaus, "The Falling Share of Profits," *Brookings Papers on Economic Activity* (1:1974).

corporate income is subject to taxation, raising the average effective rate. There is an implicit capital gain on capital purchased in prior periods at lower prices. The appropriate tax treatment of this income involves complex issues that are not central to this study. However, it is further evidence of the difficulties of specifying the correct or "right" share of profits in GNP.

Despite the uncertainties, it would be necessary to project investment in the nonenergy areas at very high levels relative to past patterns to support a view of serious problems in financing investment. Alternatively, there would have to be further and severe deterioration in profit rates, which would raise questions about the estimates of investment needs. The financing problems may be serious for the energy industries, but the sector is not large enough to move the aggregate sum of investment out of the range of past experience.

The Effects of Alternative Unemployment Rate Targets

In comparison to the previous decade, the above projections incorporate a relatively rapid rate of price inflation: the rise of the GNP deflator averages 4.7 percent annually from 1974 to 1980. However, the coupling of an equilibrium 3 percent inflation rate target with a move back to 4 percent unemployment by the end of the decade is a highly optimistic outlook. As the restrictive policies adopted in the 1973–74 inflation increased unemployment to over 7 percent, the amount of GNP growth required to reduce unemployment to 4 percent by 1980 could raise problems of imbalances and shortages similar to those of the previous expansion. An alternative projection, based on a higher unemployment rate, is illustrated in the final column of table 2-13, where unemployment is assumed to decline to only 5 percent by 1980 with the same inflation rate as in the 4 percent case.

For short-run cyclical fluctuations it has become common to associate a 3 percent loss of real output for each percentage point of increase in the unemployment rate. This more than proportionate change in output results from induced reductions in productivity growth, labor force participation, and hours worked per employee. Over the longer term, however, some of these transitory effects are moderated as hours worked and labor productivity recover from the initial decline. Thus a long-run impact on output of twice the change in unemployment appears to be more reasonable. On this basis a shift to a 5 percent unemployment goal would reduce GNP in 1980 by approximately $50 billion, slightly more than the original estimate of $43.5 billion in unallocated resources.

It would be unrealistic, however, to assume that all of this drop in demand would be in the category of unallocated resources. The lower level of output would reduce annual investment needs by several billion dollars. In addition, personal incomes would decline and therefore so would consumption. A drop in imports would act as a partial offset to these expenditure reductions. As a result of these secondary effects on other demand components, a $50 billion reduction in aggregate demand could be accomplished by lowering government expenditures (or unallocated resources) by approximately $24.5 billion.[32]

If the lower level of GNP is obtained by reducing federal government purchases, most of the net saving adjustments would be concentrated in the foreign and government sectors: the net financing position of business and households would change only slightly. Without a change in exchange rates, the fall in imports leads to an offsetting rise in net foreign investment of about $5 billion in 1980. An assumption that state and local governments maintain their baseline level of expenditures despite lower tax revenues would increase their financing gap by nearly $6 billion. On the other hand, the required reduction in federal purchases of $24.5 billion would be partially offset by an induced decline in tax revenue, estimated at $13 billion. The fall in business investment would be matched by lower retained earnings, and consumption outlays would absorb most of the change in personal income.

The federal budget position would have to be more restrictive. The budget surplus would rise by $5.5 billion if we continued to assume a transfer equal to the financing gap of state and local governments ($24.5 billion minus $13 billion minus $6 billion).[33] The magnitude of the required shift in fiscal policy, however, is more clearly illustrated by reference to a

32. This illustration is based on a simple model where the marginal federal tax rate is estimated to be 0.26 of GNP; that of state and local governments, 0.12; and corporate retained earnings, 0.10. The marginal responses of imports and investment are put at 0.10 and 0.12 respectively, and consumption is 0.94 of disposable income. The result is a multiplier for total government purchases of 2.05.

33. The $24.5 billion drop in federal purchases is partially offset by a $6 billion decline in state and local government taxes (which is covered by the federal transfer) and a $13 billion decline in federal revenue. The result is a $5.5 billion rise in the government surplus.

full employment budget surplus that does not include the induced $13 billion drop in revenue.[34] On this basis the surplus would shift from $13 billion to $31.5 billion, the net $18.5 billion change in federal expenditures. Relative to GNP the degree of fiscal restraint is slightly greater than that projected by the administration for early 1975 and is lower than that of the early 1960s. This target for resource utilization would reduce uncommitted resources to about $20 billion in 1980 ($16 billion in 1973 dollars).[35]

Potential New Programs

In recent years several studies have examined future trends in the federal budget.[36] Many foresaw serious problems in financing new programs with the revenues from the present tax structure. Higher future costs of current programs were seen as absorbing most of the revenue growth resulting from rising income. Without major changes in tax expenditure policies, the nation appeared to be committed to delaying for several years the initiation of new programs.

At first glance this study may appear to draw quite a different conclusion. The basic budget surplus is projected to reach almost $82 billion by 1980 (table 2-9). Even after a shift of $25 billion to cover the financing deficit of state and local governments, the federal government would have $57 billion for new programs. What has happened in this illustration, however, is that the government does realize a major tax increase. The

34. The full employment surplus is an estimate of the budget surplus that would prevail at a constant 4 percent unemployment rate. By eliminating induced changes in outlays and revenue associated with cyclical fluctuations in income, it focuses on the impact of tax law changes and expenditure decisions. For a detailed discussion, see Arthur M. Okun and Nancy H. Teeters, "The Full Employment Surplus Revisited," *Brookings Papers on Economic Activity* (1:1970), pp. 77–110.

35. The increased fiscal restraint is a result of the low value of the fiscal multiplier used in this illustration. This in turn follows from the nature of this exercise, in which only consumption and imports are fully determined by market forces. Residential housing and state and local government expenditures and tax rates remain unchanged for the two unemployment rates. In addition, the required size of the full employment surplus would be less if the unallocated resources were not assigned to federal government purchases. For example, a cut in taxes, while stimulating personal consumption, would shift some of the surplus in saving to the household and business sectors.

36. See, for example, Fried and others, *Setting National Priorities: The 1974 Budget*, pp. 409–41; and David J. Ott and others, *Public Claims on U.S. Output* (American Enterprise Institute for Public Policy Research, 1973), pp. 11–28.

rapid inflation of recent years and that projected for the future push people into higher tax brackets. Thus the surplus is generated by higher revenues rather than by keeping expenditures from increasing.

But the situation has not changed as much as the budget position implies. The use of the surplus as a measure of resource availability assumes that the appropriate budget is one with a zero balance: that the saving plans of households will happen to equal the net borrowing requirements of the business and foreign sectors at the target level of output. Of course, there is no reason for such a balance to occur. When private demand is weak, the federal budget—even at full employment—may have to show a substantial deficit if a target level of resource utilization is to be achieved. Conversely, when private demand is strong, the budget may have to show a substantial surplus.

Under our assumptions investment in energy programs, processing of raw materials, and pollution abatement add considerable strength to private demand. In addition, we have projected a relatively low household saving rate in response to the slow growth of after-tax income, declining inflation, and a lower unemployment rate. The scarcity is thus one of resources rather than budget dollars. The potential for new programs is measured by the $43.5 billion in unallocated resources—$19 billion if the unemployment rate is held at 5 percent.[37]

The surplus of available resources projected for the end of the decade must be viewed with great caution, as the estimate is founded on a number of crucial assumptions. The most important of these concerns the personal income tax. As incomes rise, because of real growth as well as inflation, people move into progressively higher tax brackets. This study has assumed an income elasticity of 1.5 for the federal personal income tax and at least proportional growth in other receipts. The elasticity for expenditures is slightly less than unity; hence the fiscal dividend. In the past this bonus has led to periodic tax cuts, which attempted to hold personal taxes at a constant share of incomes. It is reasonable, then, to suppose that personal tax relief may be forthcoming before 1980. Such action would cut the government budget surplus and, to a somewhat lesser extent, increase personal consumption. In our illustration, holding personal tax receipts at their 1973 share of taxable personal income would result in a $49 billion increase in consumption in 1980. This sum is larger than the $28

37. To avoid converting proposed program costs to 1980 dollars, costs in the remainder of this section are given in 1973 dollars.

billion in uncommitted resources associated with a 4 percent unemployment rate goal.

It should be pointed out, however, that real personal consumption rises by 30 percent between 1973 and 1980. In addition, the resources being withheld by the tax system from the direct control of individuals are being spent for environmental and other programs that improve the quality of life as much as consumption outlays.

Another qualification is that we have assumed no real growth in current federal programs and no unforeseen contingencies. Experience suggests that a 4 percent unemployment rate would leave little room for error in stabilization programs. Our budget assumptions may therefore be too austere and some contingency allowance might be reserved.

At the same time, several costly programs have already been included in the estimates. High levels of private investment for pollution control and energy production, residential construction in excess of household formation, and increased outlays for urban mass transit and water pollution control have been discussed. Defense spending also has been projected to climb in real terms, although some analysts foresee little or no need for real growth in this area.

Finally, substantive changes in independent programs in the welfare category (such as food stamps, supplemental security income, and the expansion of social security) combined have achieved many of the objectives of more comprehensive proposals such as the family assistance plan and the negative income tax. The costs of these programs are projected to rise sharply in the future because of increasing prices and expanded coverage.[38]

Additional resources could be freed by holding defense spending to current levels. In part, the projected growth results from an adjustment of future outlays up to the level of current obligational authority; but more increases in real terms are implicit in the projected costs of maintaining present policies. By limiting expansion of the military budget to pay and price increases, $15 billion would be added to the estimate of available resources.

New claims on resources may be warranted by 1980; here we have not taken into account the new programs that usually develop over a span of five or six years. While many programs have been proposed, only a few call for the commitment of extensive additional resources. Many, such

38. The nature of the tax system implies that low- and middle-income people will pay the costs of such transfers. This strengthens the argument for tax relief.

as tax reform or health care insurance, primarily affect the distribution of resources rather than their total quantity; they might increase claims on government budgets but not on economywide resources. Others require only small new commitments or a redirection of effort. A few new programs, however, do entail substantial resource costs.

NATIONAL HEALTH CARE INSURANCE. A number of proposals for improving health care have been advanced. The most sweeping of these are congressional efforts to develop a comprehensive national health insurance plan. The major effect of these proposals would be to change the financing mechanisms to assure an equitable distribution of the burden. Proper health care is now considered an important national goal, on a par with food, shelter, and education. Thus the costs should be apportioned according to the ability to pay rather than the degree of service required.[39] What concerns us in this study, however, is the incremental resource costs implied by the various health insurance plans under discussion. Several years ago, the Department of Health, Education, and Welfare analyzed these proposals.[40] We have extrapolated the data in that report to 1980 for two bills, one of which seems likely to be enacted: the proposal supported by the administration, which would require an additional $4.0 billion in real resources, and the earlier Kennedy-Griffiths plan, which would add $10.9 billion.[41] These amounts are for the wider coverage and increased use of medical services and products to be expected under national health insurance.

MASS TRANSIT. In an earlier section of this chapter we discussed the resources necessary, and the probable expenditure patterns, for the improvement of urban mass transit. The baseline projections incorporated an allocation for the "current funding" alternative, estimated to be $1.7 billion in 1980. Spending to meet "needs" would double that figure. Thus $1.7 billion would be the additional cost in 1980 of meeting all mass transit needs above the level of expenditures currently provided.

39. A more complete analysis of health care issues can be found in Blechman and others, *Setting National Priorities: The 1975 Budget*, chap. 8.

40. *Analysis of Health Insurance Proposals Introduced in the 92d Congress*, Printed for the Use of the Committee on Ways and Means, 92 Cong. 1 sess. (1971).

41. This assumes that without national health care insurance health care expenditures would amount to about the same percentage of GNP in 1980 as in 1972 and 1973: 7.8, 7.7, and 7.7 percent respectively. Basic data on health care expenditures may be found in Barbara S. Cooper, Nancy L. Worthington, and Paula A. Piro, "National Health Expenditures, 1929–73," and Marjorie S. Mueller, "Private Health Insurance in 1972: Health Care Services, Enrollment, and Finances," both in *Social Security Bulletin*, vol. 37 (February 1974), pp. 3–40.

INTERCITY TRANSPORTATION. One area in which increased capital investment may be envisioned is that of intercity transportation of people and goods. The nation's railroads seem particularly appropriate for improvement, given their efficient use of energy and their potential for increased capacity. Moreover, their future capital needs may be expected to greatly exceed their current spending levels, which would not be the case for air, truck, bus, or sea transportation. The estimates for rehabilitation (replacement) and expansion of rail transport systems—$2.5 billion and $1.0 billion, respectively, in 1980—are derived from government and industry projections.[42]

URBAN RENEWAL. A much discussed topic of the 1960s was government-subsidized housing and urban redevelopment. The renewal of such an effort might be considered in the last half of the 1970s. Our baseline housing projections, however, provide only for sufficient residential construction to meet the anticipated growth in household formation. A new urban renewal effort would probably affect the financing of construction and its location more than it would affect total demand.

In summary, opportunities for new programs will be severely constrained by the limited availability of resources. The combination of some tax reduction and national health care insurance would exhaust available resources unless other programs were pared down. Failure to maintain fiscal restraint would result in either a more rapid rate of inflation or the adoption of a more restrictive monetary policy than the basically accommodating one assumed here. But increasing the degree of monetary restraint by very much would make the private investment projections untenable. Furthermore, if it became necessary to follow a more gradual path in returning to full employment, the resource restrictions would become severe.

However, it should be emphasized that this projection for fiscal policy assumes that action will be taken in other areas to realize the specific goals enunciated above. Curtailing efforts in the housing, energy, or pollution abatement areas would substantially reduce investment needs. In addition, it is a projection of the average path of fiscal policy. Cyclical fluctuations in private demand might require substantial year-to-year adjustments.

42. Amounts are based on Department of Transportation, *1972 National Transportation Report*, p. xv. Estimates were derived by the capital stock method, computed from published data and using the deflator for producers' durable equipment.

CHAPTER THREE

Financial Market Implications

A FREQUENT RESPONSE to projections of future investment needs is that they cannot be financed in the capital market: observers can usually foresee growth in borrowing needs more clearly than the corresponding rise in savings. A consistent forecast of total demand in the real sector implies balanced savings and investment, but the balance may be difficult to achieve. Residential construction, for example, depends heavily on the volume of deposit funds at the major mortgage lending institutions, since the ability of home buyers to tap direct markets is extremely limited. In turn, the growth of deposits at these institutions is dependent on savings in the household sector and the relation between market interest rates and deposit rates. A projection that incorporates monetary restraint will result in low deposit growth, limited mortgage availability, and a low level of residential construction. The same projection for the gross national product could be realized with greater fiscal restraint and an easing of monetary policy, with a consequent increase in funds for mortgage financing.

The capital market projections that follow are based on the investment and savings data of the previous chapter. It is assumed that fiscal restraint is sufficient to permit a shift toward an easier monetary policy, which is needed if financial intermediaries are to have the funds to meet projected residential mortgage demand. In addition, the derivation of a capital market projection requires that the unallocated resources be assigned to a specific sector's expenditures. For simplicity, these resources were added to personal consumption, with a reduction of federal personal income taxes sufficient to maintain the previous saving rates. Also, federal grants to state and local governments were raised by an amount equal to their operating account deficit, as outlined in tables 2-13 and 2-14. These two modifications reduce the federal budget surplus to $9.5 billion in 1980. The increase in grants is of little consequence; we could just as well have specified an increase in state and local taxes offset by a federal tax reduction. Assignment of the unallocated resources to expenditures other than consumption would change the capital market implications only slightly. The significant point is that there would still be a surplus even after the financing needs of state and local governments had been met and all resources had been allocated.[1]

The size and composition of the borrowing needs of the major investment sectors are examined in greater detail in the next four sections. The substantial growth of business external financing is offset here by much lower levels of government borrowing than those of recent years. One result of this financing shift is that the outstanding marketable debt will be increasingly concentrated in longer-term maturities. This may increase the attractiveness of certificates of deposit and commercial paper as primary liquidity instruments and place upward pressure on long-term interest rates.

The role of financial intermediaries is examined in the fifth section, and a balancing of the supply of and demand for direct market credit instruments is derived. An easier monetary policy than that of the first part of the decade results in a rapid expansion of financial intermediation. Most of the growth of credit market debt is absorbed by the intermediaries and exchanged for the more liquid deposit accounts of households.

The high levels of business investment are financed by a sharp shift in the federal budget toward restraint, offset in part by the relaxation of monetary policy. The federal surplus is redirected into the capital markets and provides a major portion of the increased saving necessary to finance investment. Since such a shift of the policy mix is problematic, we also examine the effects of a more expansionary fiscal policy combined with sufficient monetary restraint to hold aggregate demand at the previous

1. This surplus is smaller than that shown in table 2-13 because the assignment of the unallocated resources to personal consumption instead of government purchases requires a larger tax reduction to offset the increment to personal saving.

target level. In this case, most studies imply that private investment would bear the brunt of adjustment, with the relatively minor side effect of higher interest rates on saving.

Finally, the implications for U.S. capital markets of the recent rise in oil prices are examined. Because the revenues of the oil exporting countries will greatly exceed their import capacity, they will be investing large amounts in the oil importing countries. The task of redirecting this surplus back to individual deficit nations may result in an expanded role for the United States as an international financial intermediary. The large trade deficit of the oil consuming industrial countries will also restrain the growth of their aggregate demand. Although an expansion of private capital investment has done much to offset its effect, the existence of such a trade deficit would moderate the need for large federal budget surpluses.

Capital market projections are inherently subject to even greater error than those of the real sector. These instruments are highly fungible, and the past has shown that institutional adjustments occur much more quickly in the financial markets. Most problems of the capital markets have been associated with cycles of monetary imbalance rather than secular changes; these cyclical strains result from the financing of long-term assets by short-term liabilities of the financial intermediaries. The rapid growth of long-term bond financing projected here implies that such cyclical problems will become more severe unless institutional changes are allowed to bring the two sides of the balance sheet into closer alignment.[2]

Housing Finance

Home building requirements for the rest of this decade, as discussed earlier, are projected to be only slightly above the rate of 1971–73. These projections can give some indication of the level of mortgage loan demand, but the relation between investment and borrowing is not one-to-one.

2. The projections of this chapter are based in part on the results of a capital market model of the authors: Barry Bosworth and James S. Duesenberry, "A Flow of Funds Model and Its Implications," in *Issues in Federal Debt Management*, Proceedings of a Conference held by the Federal Reserve Bank of Boston, June 1973. However, we have made extensive use of the techniques outlined by Stephen P. Taylor in "Long-term Prospects for Housing Finance: A Projection to 1980," in *Ways to Moderate Fluctuations in Housing Construction* (Board of Governors of the Federal Reserve System, 1972), pp. 432–55.

Nor is it a constant ratio over time because of the influence of rising site costs, changing loan terms, and the refinancing under inflationary conditions of the existing housing stock. Two methods have been used to account for these factors, yielding slightly different projections of loan requirements.

In the Taylor study a flow method was used to project mortgage demand through 1980.[3] The method was based primarly on the anticipated ratio of net borrowing to new construction. Taylor projected (1) an annual average of 2.3 million starts (excluding mobile homes and rehabilitations); (2) a constant real value per unit and a constant rate of inflation (3.4 percent); (3) single-family houses equal to 58 percent of the total; and (4) a ratio of net mortgage accumulation to construction values slightly above that of the early 1960s. This method gave an outstanding mortgage stock of $737 billion in 1980.

Using Taylor's methods but correcting for higher rates of inflation and our lower level of starts yielded a projected mortgage stock of $847 billion. This figure is 15 percent higher than Taylor's estimate because of a higher projected rate of increase in construction costs and a much higher than anticipated ratio of mortgage flows to construction expenditures in the three years since his estimates were made.[4]

The projections based on a flow demand for mortgages assume the maintenance of a stable relation between mortgages for new construction and new mortgages on the existing stock. The reasonableness of this assumption is most questionable in periods of rapid inflation, when the refinancing of existing housing adds large increments to the mortgage stock.

An alternative approach to projecting mortgage demand is the stock method, which involves estimating a ratio of debt to real estate value (housing stock plus site value) and applying this ratio to projections of

3. Taylor, "Long-term Prospects for Housing Finance." The flow approach is also illustrated by David S. Huang, "Effect of Different Credit Policies on Housing Demand," in Irwin Friend (director), *Study of the Savings and Loan Industry*, submitted to the Federal Home Loan Bank Board (U.S. Government Printing Office, 1970), vol. 3, pp. 1211–39, and in the *Second Annual Report on National Housing Goals,* Message from the President of the United States, 91 Cong. 2 sess. (1970).

4. The magnitude of this revised figure clearly indicates the importance of the inflation projection underlying long-term projections in nominal terms. However, the economic implications of inflation are less important since, in the long run, income, savings, and investment increase by roughly proportionate amounts.

Table 3-1. *Value of Residential Real Estate and Mortgage Stock, End of Selected Years, 1960–80*

Description	1960	1965	1970	1973[a]	1980[b]
Value of residential real estate (billions of dollars)	488	631	864	1,165	2,181
Ratio of real estate debt to value	0.332	0.396	0.391	0.409	0.388[c]
					0.416[d]
Residential mortgage stock					
Value (billions of dollars)	162	250	338	476	847[c]
					908[d]
Annual rate of growth from this year to year in next column (percent)	9.1	6.2	12.1	8.6[c]	...
					9.7[d]

Sources: See the appendix.
a. Preliminary.
b. Projected.
c. Assumes a debt–value ratio flow for each component of residential structures (the flow method described in the text).
d. Assumes a 1973 debt–value ratio for each component of residential structures (the stock method described in the text).

housing stock value in 1980.[5] This ratio has been much higher for apartments than for single-family houses because tax laws favor apartment house owners with high mortgage debt. However, the two ratios have followed the same trend since 1948: a steady rise before 1965 and a fall during the ensuing years of tight credit. The historical pattern of the overall debt–value ratio is shown in table 3-1.

Recent monetary conditions have also caused wide swings in the debt–value ratio. Periods of high interest rates slowed mortgage flows while the value of the housing stock increased. In addition, the mortgage stock

5. This approach follows a methodology outlined by James Wetzler, "Forecasting Mortgage Demand" (Harvard University, 1972; processed). We obtained depreciation rate assumptions and an initial real stock estimate from Allan H. Young, John C. Musgrave, and Claudia Harkins, "Residential Capital in the United States, 1925–70," Department of Commerce, *Survey of Current Business*, vol. 51 (November 1971), pp. 16–27. The constant dollar stock was multiplied by the residential construction deflator and adjusted by a Federal Housing Administration site–value ratio reported in U.S. Department of Housing and Urban Development, *1971 HUD Statistical Yearbook* (1972). The resulting measure of real estate value is lower than that of census estimates, but the differences appear to be relatively constant, and the stock method allows using a straightforward methodology for projection. Site costs as a percentage of value are assumed to rise at the 1960–70 trend rate. Separate calculations are made for structures housing one to four families and for structures of more than five units.

appears to respond more slowly to inflation in the price of existing homes than to increases in the physical stock. The sharp rise in the ratios during the boom years of 1971–73 offers some evidence that the ratios were depressed during the late 1960s.

The lengthening maturity of mortgage loans provides a partial explanation for the postwar rise in the debt–value ratio.[6] Little further gain would result from lengthening mortgage maturity as a means of lowering monthly payments because an even larger part of them would be consumed by interest costs. Thus a projection that in the long run the ratio of debt to real estate value will level off seems reasonable. If the ratios returned to their depressed levels of 1969, the residential mortgage stock would total $865 billion in 1980. A more realistic forecast, holding the ratios to their 1973 level, is consistent with the credit conditions assumed in the projections of housing starts and implies a mortgage stock of $908 billion. This is about 7 percent above the comparable flow projections.

These projections indicate a strong, but not unmanageable, demand for mortgages during the rest of this decade. The estimate of starts in relation to demographic trends seems generous if one accepts the growing importance of mobile homes as not being inconsistent with other aspects of housing policy. The resulting figures for residential construction represent a smaller percentage of GNP than was maintained in the 1960s. The existing ratio of debt to real estate value does not mean there is a huge backlog of mortgage demand for financing the inflation of home values that has already occurred. The average annual growth of 9.7 percent in the mortgage stock between 1973 and 1980 exceeds the growth rate of the 1960s but is substantially below the 1970–73 boom. Much of the growth in credit demand results from inflation and will be matched by a corresponding growth in the funds entering the capital markets.

Capital Financing of State and Local Governments

The borrowing requirements of state and local governments are closely tied to their capital financing because of the restrictions on operating fund deficits. After declining in real terms in recent years, capital outlays are expected to grow rapidly for the remainder of the decade—particu-

---

6. Much of the rise was due to the resale at postwar prices of houses that were mortgage-free at the end of World War II.

Table 3-2. *Capital Formation of State and Local Governments, Methods
of Financing, and Debt, Selected Years, 1960–80*

Billions of dollars

Description	1960	1965	1970	1973[a]	1980[b]
Gross capital formation[c]	15.0	22.2	31.3	35.6	66.6
Methods of financing					
Federal capital grants	3.0	4.5	6.2	8.0	17.1
Bond issues	7.3	10.5	18.1	22.4	33.0
Other financing	4.7	7.2	7.0	5.2	16.5
Outstanding debt[d]	70.8	100.3	144.5	181.9	292.0
Long-term	67.3	94.8	131.2	167.3	275.0
Short-term	3.5	5.5	13.3	14.6	17.0

Sources: See the appendix. The data used here differ from the construction data used in table 2-5 because of the inclusion here of margins on used structures and of construction force account compensation.
a. Preliminary.
b. Projected.
c. Excludes purchases of land.
d. End of year.

larly for transportation and environmental programs. But these expenditures will not lead to a proportionate growth of bond financing.

Historically, bond issues have financed over 50 percent of capital outlays, with the remainder being financed from operating account revenues. In recent years, however, federal grants for capital programs have increased greatly—from less than $1 billion in 1955 to $8 billion in 1973, which represented 22 percent of capital formation. The nonhighway portion of these grants will rise rapidly because of federal support for waste treatment and mass transportation projects. In addition, the composition of state and local capital formation is shifting away from education, where local bond financing has dominated, toward the grant-supported programs. As shown in table 3-2, capital grants are estimated to amount to 26 percent of capital outlays in 1980. The easing of pressure on current operating budgets and the continuation of general revenue sharing should also help end the decline in the share of financing from other revenue sources.

As a result of the above factors, new bond issues for capital financing are projected to grow at an annual rate of 6.2 percent between 1973 and 1980 while total capital formation grows at 8.2 percent. This increase in debt issues is less than the 10 percent annual increase in state and local government tax revenue. The total amount of debt would rise at a 7.0

percent annual rate; in the 1960s it rose at 7.4 percent and during the capital expenditure boom of the 1950s at 11.2 percent.

Business Financing Needs

The proportion of business capital outlays financed by external borrowing has been very high since the middle of the 1960s. Net external financing averaged 23 percent of capital outlays from 1966 to 1973 but only 11 percent for the first half of the 1960s (see figure 3-1). This resulted from both a decline in internal funds as a share of GNP and a rise in the proportion of output devoted to capital formation. A similar pattern of strong demand for external funds is projected here for the rest of the 1970s: a slight improvement in internal funds as a share of GNP is more than offset by substantial increases in capital outlays. Net external financing needs will average $64.6 billion annually through 1980—almost twice the annual average of $33.9 billion for 1971–73. As a share of total capital uses, however, this is a fairly modest increase and is below the levels for some individual years, such as 1950, 1951, and 1970.

A brief outline of prospective changes in the business balance sheet is shown in table 3-3. During the 1960s the financing of the external deficit was made easier by substantial economies in the use of liquid assets, which declined sharply relative to measures of economic activity such as GNP. This trend was reversed during the first three years of the 1970s as business firms increased their borrowing beyond what was needed for capital outlays in order to raise their liquid asset reserves. A continuing decline in the ratio of liquid assets to GNP, however, is projected through 1980. The magnitude of the statistical discrepancy for the business flow-of-funds account is a second factor complicating the determination of total borrowing requirements. In table 3-3 this is allocated to the residual asset category, together with net trade credit and a few residual financial asset items.

Total borrowing by business is projected to average $108 billion a year from 1974 to 1980, whereas from 1971 to 1973 the average was $78 billion. This is an 8.8 percent annual growth in the outstanding stock of liabilities versus 8.5 percent in 1966–73. Thus while the numbers are large they are not very different from those that the capital market has had to absorb in past years. Long-term borrowing is projected to amount

Figure 3-1. *Business External Financing, Actual, 1970–73, and Projected, 1974–80*

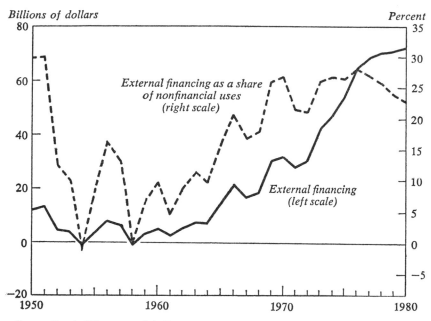

Billions of dollars   *Percent*

External financing as a share
of nonfinancial uses
(right scale)

External financing
(left scale)

Sources: Board of Governors of the Federal Reserve System, "Flow of Funds Accounts, 1945–1972" (1973; processed), and "Flow of Funds, Unadjusted, 4th Quarter, 1973, Preliminary" (February 8, 1974; processed). The specific table and line sources from "Flow of Funds" are the same as for table 3-3 below, first and third lines (see the appendix).

to approximately the same proportion as in previous years. We have assumed that corporate stock issues will follow the pattern of the last few years and reflect a growing concern about the financial burden of rising debt. The rise of residential mortgage debt results from the growth in multifamily housing. Commercial mortgages are easily interchangeable with private bond issues since they differ only in having a specific asset for collateral. Bank loans are projected to continue as the dominant source of short-term credit although not at the rapid growth rate of recent years.

This is not to imply that business financing needs will be unmanageable during the rest of the 1970s, unless one believes that the borrowing rate of 1966–73 is not sustainable. Alternatively, levels of investment even higher than those specified in chapter 2 are possible. It seems more likely, however, that questions of profitability and availability of resources in

Table 3-3. *Investment, Financing, and Assets of the Business Sector,*[a]
Selected Periods, 1961–80

Billions of dollars, annual averages

Description	1961–65	1966–70	1971–73	1974–80[b]
Business investment[c]				
Total	72.3	110.6	146.5	251.5
Internal financing	64.6	86.5	112.6	186.9
External financing needed	7.7	24.1	33.9	64.6
External funds raised				
Long-term	14.4	28.0	54.3	75.3
Corporate bonds	5.7	15.4	18.4	33.2
Corporate stock	0.8	2.8	10.4	12.3
Commercial mortgages	4.4	5.6	13.8	15.3
Residential mortgages	3.5	4.3	11.7	14.5
Short-term	8.0	14.8	25.5	35.5
Bank loans	6.8	10.3	23.0	28.9
Open market paper	1.2	4.7	2.5	6.6
Assets accumulated[d]				
Liquid	3.1	2.3	11.9	6.0
Consumer credit	2.9	2.4	5.9	7.3
Residual[e]	8.7	14.2	27.9	32.9

Sources: See the appendix. Figures are rounded.
a. The business sector includes all nonfinancial business and finance companies.
b. Projected.
c. Investment and internal financing follow the definition of table 2-13, with the addition of direct foreign investment.
d. Total external financing minus assets equals external financing needed.
e. Residual assets include net trade credit, residual financial asset items, and statistical discrepancy.

the real sector will be a constraining factor than that capital markets will be unable to service financing needs.

The Federal Government

The strong demand projected for real resources in the private sector, discussed in the previous chapter, implies that there must be a surplus in the federal budget for the remainder of the decade. In addition, as shown in table 3-4, we have projected only a slight increase in government loans as foreign lending is reduced and other loan programs are converted to loan guarantees or moved outside the budget. This shift in the budget position contrasts sharply with that of past years, when budget deficits were the cause of heavy federal borrowing.

Table 3-4. *Financial Transactions of the Federal Government Sector,*[a] *Selected Periods, 1961–80*

Billions of dollars, average annual flows

Item or transaction	1961–65	1966–70	1971–73	1974–80[b]
Budget deficit	1.8	4.5	12.5	−11.5
Total assets	3.9	7.7	15.2	9.0
Federal Home Loan Bank advances to savings and loan associations	0.8	0.9	1.5	1.3
Residential mortgages of Federal National Mortgage Association and other agencies	−0.3	3.6	6.2	2.2
Official foreign reserve assets	−0.8	−0.4	−1.3	0.0
Loans to foreigners	1.2	1.7	1.8	0.5
Other loans and adjustments (net)[c]	3.0	1.9	7.0	5.0
Total liabilities	5.7	12.2	27.7	−2.5
Unborrowed reserves	0.6	1.4	1.6	4.0
Currency	1.5	2.6	4.2	5.0
Credit market debt	3.6	8.2	21.9	−11.5

Sources: See the appendix.
a. Includes the federal government, sponsored credit agencies, and the Federal Reserve System.
b. Projected.
c. Includes minor financial assets and liabilities, unpaid tax liabilities, and statistical discrepancy.

Loans of the sponsored credit agencies are a second source of increased issues of government debt. These agencies can be viewed as financial intermediaries in that they exchange federal debt for different types of private debt instruments. Agency lending does not result in a net increase of market debt, but agency operations do affect its composition. Most of the agency support is directed toward the mortgage market. We have assumed that advances of the Federal Home Loan Banks to savings and loan associations will continue at the high levels of recent years and average 4.5 percent of savings and loan deposits for the remainder of the decade. These advances rise from $15 billion at the end of 1973 to $24 billion in 1980. Direct mortgage acquisitions of the Federal National Mortgage Association and other agencies are assumed to equal the difference between the projected demand for mortgage funds and those supplied by private lenders. Under our assumption of a relatively easy monetary policy, the agency holdings of residential mortgages rise from $35.8 billion in 1973 to $51 billion in 1980. Some growth can be anticipated in other agency lending programs such as the Student Loan Marketing Association and the Farm Credit Administration. These loans are projected to rise by $2.5 billion a year.

Open market operations of the Federal Reserve are the final determinant of changes in the publicly held debt. We have assumed that future increases in the money supply will be met by raising the supply of reserves rather than through reductions in reserve requirements. These reserves are allowed to grow at an annual average rate of 9.1 percent between 1973 and 1980 while GNP grows at 10.3 percent. Because of the absorption of reserves by time deposits, the money supply grows at a lower rate. Growth in the currency component of the money supply at an average rate of 6.5 percent is an additional offset to increases in public debt issues.

Under the above assumptions, net federal credit claims are projected to decline during the remainder of the decade, representing a sharp break with recent trends such as the average annual increase of $13.3 billion in the outstanding stock of credit market liabilities from 1965 to 1973. This reduced federal borrowing is a major offset to the projected expansion of business debt. The slower growth follows directly from the assumed budget surplus and monetary conditions sufficiently easy to enable the deposit institutions to meet the demand for mortgage funds without extensive government support.

Table 3-5 shows the distribution of credit market borrowing. Although the total issues and the total increase in the holdings are balanced, the federal government is shown as a negative net issuer, since the nonfederal securities acquired by the various holders add up to $117.6 billion a year. At the same time the various holders are reducing their holdings of federal securities by $11.5 billion for a total net accumulation of $106.1 billion a year. Some further change in the relative yields of private and federal securities will be required to bring about the shift. Domestic holdings of federal securities other than those of savings banks are already relatively small—only $137 billion—of which commercial banks hold about 40 percent. Ordinary market forces will readily bring about some reduction in the holdings of households, corporations, and state and local governments, but special measures may be required to bring about the full required shift without disrupting financial markets. Advance refundings of long-term issues or switches in the Federal Reserve portfolio would minimize the loss of liquidity to the financial systems. Elimination of the savings bond program would also be helpful. In the absence of special measures, short Treasury securities will become increasingly scarce and

Table 3-5. *Borrowing in the Credit Markets,*[a] *Selected Periods, 1961–80*

Billions of dollars, average annual flows

Issuer or holder	1961–65	1966–70	1971–73	1974–80
Issuer of credit				
Federal government[b]	3.6	8.2	21.9	−11.5
Nonfinancial business	19.0	38.6	68.1	96.3
State and local governments	5.9	8.8	12.5	15.7
Foreign investors	2.0	1.2	3.5	3.6
Commercial banks	0.4	0.6	1.6	2.0
Total	30.8	57.4	107.6	106.1
Holder of credit				
Commercial banks	14.0	20.9	43.6	54.1
Nonbank intermediaries[c]	5.8	8.9	23.1	33.1
Nonfinancial business	0.8	0.7	6.4	1.4
State and local governments	0.8	1.9	0.3	4.2
Foreign investors	0.7	3.1	14.2	5.0
Households and others	8.7	21.9	19.7	8.3
Total	30.8	57.4	107.6	106.1

Sources: See the appendix. Figures are rounded.

a. Includes all bonds, corporate stock, commercial mortgages, government securities, and bank loans; excludes residential mortgages and consumer credit.

b. Net of U.S. government agency securities, sponsored credit agencies, and the Federal Reserve System.

c. Savings and loan associations, mutual savings banks, and life insurance companies.

their yields will decline relative to other short instruments. New liquidity instruments can undoubtedly be developed to replace them.

The Role of the Mortgage Lending Institutions

The residential mortgage market is dominated by three types of institutions—savings and loan associations, mutual savings banks, and commercial banks which together held 73 percent of the outstanding stock in 1973, and accounted for 89 percent of the net growth in privately held mortgages between 1965 and 1973. These institutions occupy a very favorable position in the mortgage market. Only they have the local offices required for servicing such loans; and by combining their local deposit and loan activities they realize economies not available to nationally oriented institutions. For example, life insurance companies, which were formerly significant contributors of funds, have reduced their holdings of residential mortgages in favor of higher-yield corporate debt issues. Innovations have been made by the government to encourage a broader lending base in the mortgage market, but the volume of other private lending remains small.

The dependence of the mortgage market on deposit institutions is a major source of its instability. Because these institutions lend long (mortgages) and borrow short (deposits), their operations have been frequently disrupted by the gyrations in monetary policy since 1966. Earnings on a loan portfolio acquired when rates were lower have been inadequate to pay the rates required to attract deposits in the face of rising yields on competing assets. The problem has been made worse by rate ceilings, which restrict the institutions that might otherwise have paid a higher dividend.

If the increases in competing market rates were purely cyclical around a constant level, they could be met by drawing down reserves with a subsequent rebuilding during periods of declining rates. But market rates have shown a marked upward trend since 1965, and the duration and magnitude of cyclical highs have strained the institutions' reserves.[7]

The relation between current market yields on assets and the institutions' dividend payments shown in figure 3-2 is not a simple one. First, the gross portfolio yield responds only slowly to changing market rates. Mortgage loans are written for as long as thirty years, although early repayment and refinancing shorten the actual average lag; and annual repayments have ranged between 10 and 15 percent of the outstanding stock. Only about half of the adjustment to a one-time change in the market rate is completed within five years. Second, operating expenses have reduced net operating income by 1.1 to 1.2 percent of total assets over the last twenty years. Finally, not all of net income is available for dividends since a portion must go into reserves. Thus in the long run

---

7. It has been amply demonstrated by previous articles that the profit-maximizing institution should pay a dividend based on existing market yields, not on its existing portfolio earnings. See, for example, Stephen M. Goldfeld and Dwight M. Jaffee, "The Determinants of Deposit-Rate Setting by Savings and Loan Associations," *Journal of Finance*, vol. 25 (June 1970), pp. 615–32. This does not alter the fact that such associations have suffered a capital loss on their existing fixed yield portfolios because of market rate increases and that an existing institution can pay total dividends in excess of net income only on a temporary basis. Because of the limited entry of new competitors into local markets, the rate elasticity of deposit demand may be low enough to prevent the institution's bankruptcy. As shown by the experience of savings and loan associations before the rate ceilings of 1966, disintermediation is not a problem caused solely by the existence of such ceilings.

Figure 3-2. *Interest Rates Paid and Received by Savings and Loan Associations, and Income as a Percentage of the Value of Assets, 1955–73*

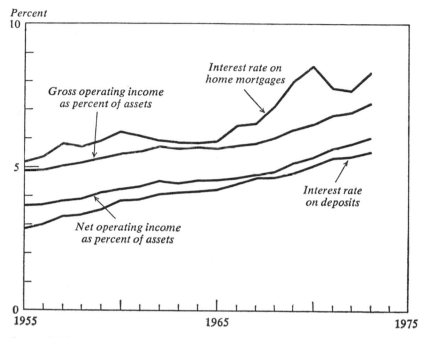

Sources: U.S. League of Savings Association, *1974 Savings and Loan Fact Book;* and Board of Governors of the Federal Reserve System, *Federal Reserve Bulletin,* various issues, table of mortgage interest rate yields—FHA series for new homes.

savings and loan associations can remain viable with an average deposit rate about 1.25 to 1.5 percent below mortgage market rates.

In future years the deposit institutions will be in a position to supply substantial funds to the mortgage market, even at the interest rates that prevailed during the credit crunches of previous years. This is because the higher market rates that occurred in the last half of the 1960s are now showing up in portfolio yields of the financial intermediaries. The gross yield on assets of savings and loan associations, for example, rose from 5.7 percent in 1965 to 7.2 percent in 1973. Also, the institutions' ability to match competing rates has been much improved by diversifying the type of deposit accounts they offer. Higher rates can be offered to the more rate-sensitive depositors without a proportionate increase in total interest payments. In 1972 yields on certificate accounts of one-year maturity reached 5.75 percent whereas the average payout was 5.4 percent. In mid-1973 the rate ceilings were revised to allow rates from 6.5 percent for one-year accounts to 7.5 percent for maturities in excess of four years. For the deposit institutions, the important consideration is the pace at which market rates change. Sudden cyclical increases in rates such as that of 1973–74 will continue to cause problems. But over the longer term portfolio yields adjust. Since market rates in our projections decline from their 1974 peaks, the institutions encounter few difficulties in maintaining a high deposit growth rate.

The competition for credit among the financial intermediaries is another potential source of concern for the mortgage market. Regulatory restrictions prevent savings and loan associations and mutual savings banks from holding as diversified an asset portfolio as commercial banks. They are not able to adjust as quickly to rising market rates because their asset structure is dominated by longer-term mortgage loans. Thus, if they are not constrained by deposit rate ceilings, commercial banks can offer higher deposit rates during periods of tight monetary restraint with the result that funds are drawn away from the mortgage market toward business loans.

The Competition for Credit

It is our conclusion that the combinations of credit demands outlined above can be financed without serious problems. But several important assumptions must be made. The major burden of stabilization policy is assumed to fall on fiscal policy with a budget surplus being maintained throughout 1974–80. This allows monetary policy to follow a generally accommodating path. Together with an assumed gradual reduction in the inflation rate the monetary policy results in a decline of interest rates from their 1974 peaks to levels more comparable to 1968 and 1971–72 with a Treasury bill rate of 5.0 to 5.5 percent. However, long-term market rates remain at relatively high levels because of a concentration of capital market borrowing at the end of the maturity distribution. The projected term structure of interest rates is similar to that of 1970–73 when short-term rates fell far more than bond rates. The corporate Baa rate is projected to decline slowly to about 8 percent.

The composition of direct market borrowing by issuer and holder was shown in table 3-5. The high levels of business borrowing are largely offset by a slower growth of state and local government debt and a decline in the volume of publicly held federal debt. As a result, the annual average of total net issues from 1974 to 1980 is below that of 1971–73.

On the demand side of the market the drop in competing market rates results in a substantial increase in financial intermediation. The household sector, in particular, channels more of its investment through the deposit institutions. Commercial banks and the three major nonbank intermediaries absorb over 80 percent of the growth in direct market debt as against 52 percent in 1966–70.

There is a substantial rise in residential mortgage demand during the rest of the decade, but because a large portion represents refinancing of existing homes it does not create a net claim on savings. For the household sector as a whole, the rise in the mortgage liabilities of home buyers is matched by a rise in the financial assets of sellers. In other words, the increase in mortgage debt is financed by a corresponding increase in net financial asset accumulation.

As shown in table 3-6, the lending institutions are able to meet the assumed demand for residential mortgage credit with very little intervention by the government agencies because the ceiling rates on deposit accounts have little effect as short-term rates decline. In addition, the yield on existing loan portfolios has almost adjusted to several years of high mortgage rates. Thus the problem of generating sufficient operating income to meet interest payments will be less severe.

The mortgage rate is projected to remain below comparable corporate bond yields. This reversal of the traditional interest difference between mortgages and bonds developed in the early 1970s and is assumed to continue because of heavy business borrowing in the long-term bond markets. Legal restrictions on portfolio composition prevent savings and loan associations and mutual savings banks from fully arbitraging mortgages and bonds, so the relative quantities of assets in the two markets do have an influence on the rate structure. The residential mortgage market, however, becomes increasingly dominated by these two types of deposit institutions as life insurance companies and commercial banks direct a larger proportion of their funds into the direct market to take advantage of higher yields. The two kinds of deposit institutions absorb nearly 85 percent of the growth from 1974 to 1980 in mortgage debt as against 53 percent from 1966 to 1970.

Most of the projected growth of credit market debt is in long-term

Table 3-6. *Changes in Liabilities and Assets of Financial Intermediaries,*[a] *Selected Periods, 1961–80*

Billions of dollars, average annual flows

Description	1961–65	1966–70	1971–73	1974–80[b]
Commercial banks				
Deposit accounts	19.6	25.7	58.9	76.4
Assets				
Residential mortgages	2.4	2.6	9.5	7.3
Credit market holdings[c]	14.0	20.9	43.6	54.1
Consumer credit	3.9	4.8	11.9	15.5
Savings and loan associations				
Deposit accounts	9.7	7.2	27.1	46.7
Assets				
Residential mortgages	8.9	7.3	24.1	38.1
Credit market holdings[c]	1.7	1.5	6.6	9.4
Mutual savings banks				
Deposit accounts	3.2	3.8	8.3	17.5
Assets				
Residential mortgages	3.2	2.0	3.6	13.7
Credit market holdings[c]	0.0	1.5	3.7	4.5
Life insurance companies				
Reserves[d]	5.2	5.9	10.6	17.5
Assets				
Residential mortgages	1.9	0.9	−0.9	−0.7
Credit market holdings[c]	4.1	5.9	12.7	19.1
Addenda				
Residential mortgages, total[e]	17.7	17.6	46.1	61.9
Federal Home Loan Bank advances	0.8	0.9	1.5	1.3
Federal National Mortgage Association purchases of residential mortgages	−0.1	2.8	6.4	2.2

Sources: See the appendix.
a. Excludes noncredit market assets and liabilities except residential mortgages and consumer credit.
b. Projected.
c. See table 3-5, note a, for a list of the assets included under credit market holdings.
d. Policy reserves are deducted from reserves.
e. Includes government and privately held mortgages as well as those held by financial institutions.

corporate and state and local government securities. The federal government, under the policies assumed in this study, would experience a decline in its net debt outstanding. Since most of the growth of federal debt has been in the short-maturity categories, this pattern of borrowing needs indicates that marketable short-term liquid assets may become relatively scarce. Such a situation could result in a rapid expansion of negotiable certificates of deposit and commercial paper to meet the need for such instruments.

The state and local government debt increase can be met without difficulty by commercial banks and people with high incomes. The expansion of long-term corporate debt, however, will be more difficult to place. The net growth is too great to be absorbed by life insurance companies and pension funds—the traditional holders of such securities. But individuals are usually reluctant to hold long-term securities except at substantial premiums. The increasing prevalence in the primary security markets of long-term securities emphasizes the importance of financial intermediaries that will exchange long-term assets for short-term liquid deposit liabilities, which are more attractive to individual savers.

The Implications of Alternative Policy Combinations

In this study we have specified a much more restrictive federal budget than those of the early part of the decade, offset by an easing of monetary policy. Since a shift in the budget surplus of the magnitude required may be difficult to achieve, we also discuss briefly the implications of a policy mix that relies more heavily on monetary restraint. Several aspects of this alternative can be examined by focusing on the shift in the composition of aggregate demand that would result from a $10 billion increase in federal government purchases and a decrease in unborrowed reserves sufficient to leave the GNP unchanged.[8] These policy adjustments are illustrated in table 3-7.

The original increase in government spending raises consumption through increasing disposable income. Business investment needs also increase because of accelerator effects from the high level of output. However, the increased business and government borrowing, if not accommodated by growth of the monetary aggregates, would raise market rates and draw funds away from the residential housing market. The response of imports to higher levels of domestic demand reduces the net trade balance.

Now, if monetary restraint is to return aggregate demand to its earlier

8. The specific illustration of table 3-7 is based on a flow-of-funds model of the authors, but the general conclusions are the same for other econometric models of more general use. Because it allows for induced changes in state and local expenditures, the model incorporates a larger multiplier than in table 2-13. The results will differ somewhat according to the amount of time that is allowed to elapse after the original policy change because of the interaction of lags, accelerator responses in investment, and multiplier effects. This discussion focuses on an intermediate period of the third-year adjustments.

Table 3-7. *Distribution of the Impact on Demand of a $10 Billion Increase in Federal Expenditures, Offset by a Decrease in Unborrowed Reserves, by Major Category*

Billions of constant dollars

| | Distribution of change in gross national product[a] | | |
Demand category	Increase in federal purchases	Reduction in unborrowed reserves	Net effect
Personal consumption	13.5	−11.3	2.2
Business investment	5.9	−12.4	−6.5
Residential construction	−1.1	−2.4	−3.5
Net exports	−1.3	1.3	0.0
Purchases, state and local governments	0	−2.2	−2.2
Purchases, federal government	10.0	0	10.0
Gross national product	27.0	−27.0	0.0

Sources: See the appendix.
a. The results shown here are the third-year multiplier effects of a $10 billion stimulus to constant dollar government purchases and a reduction in unborrowed reserves (calculated as $1.25 billion) sufficient to leave GNP unchanged. The bond rate would increase by 200 basis points.

level, it must do so primarily by raising market interest rates. In this example, a $10 billion rise in federal purchases would require reducing unborrowed reserves by about $1.25 billion and increasing the corporate bond rate by 200 basis points. The initial effects of this policy are concentrated in the interest-sensitive areas of residential construction, business investment, and state and local governments' capital outlays. Federal expenditures are not much affected and the impact on consumption is limited to the secondary repercussions of a fall in income.

The net effect of these two policy changes is to raise federal spending and consumption but to lower investment. The precise amounts involved are uncertain and depend on which period after the policy changes one examines. However, this shift would clearly make it more difficult to achieve the goals for capital expenditures outlined in chapter 2.

The Implications of Alternative Inflation Rates

The inflation-unemployment assumptions of this study are highly optimistic about the resolution of the nation's current economic problems. In the previous chapter some of the probable effects of a higher (5 percent) rate of unemployment were examined. Variations in the rate of price inflation were of less direct importance since both nominal income and expenditures of the major sectors rise by roughly proportionate amounts. In the capital market, however, the rate of inflation is of greater importance because of its impact on nominal interest rates. Even with constant real rates of interest, changes in nominal rates alter the distribution of credit and thus of real resources.

The institutional structure of the financial intermediaries illustrates the problem of adjusting to changes in nominal rates. The concentration of the deposit institutions' assets in long-term fixed-yield securities delays the response of their income to changes in market rates. Even without deposit rate ceilings, their ability to match market rates in the competition for deposit funds is severely strained whenever interest rates are pushed above their rate of net operating income. The result is slow deposit growth, limited mortgage availability, and declining residential construction.

The process of "disintermediation" is of no importance in the basic projections of this chapter because nominal short-term interest rates fall to levels below the net portfolio yield of the principal mortgage lending institutions. But this pattern of interest rates is crucially dependent on a moderation of the inflation and greater fiscal restraint as a substitute for the present monetary stringency.

Some of the structural problems that might be encountered in the capital markets are illustrated if we assume a more rapid price inflation, 6.5 percent a year for the rest of the decade rather than the 4.5 percent rate of the basic projections. If this inflation were fully reflected in nominal rates, they would be raised by two percentage points—a corporate bond Baa rate of 9.5 to 10 percent and short-term rates in the range of 7 to 8 percent at the end of the decade. If mortgage interest rates should stay above 9 percent until 1980, the income of savings and loan institutions would gradually rise, as their mortgage holdings turned over, to the point where they could afford to pay a better average dividend, 6.75 to 7 percent in 1980, than the 5.6 percent rate of 1973. This would allow them to offer rates in the range of about 7.5 percent for certificates maturing in one to two years—a deposit category dominated by more interest-sensitive accounts. These rates are less than one percentage point above the deposit rates of the basic projections, and the mortgage institutions would lose their assumed rate advantage over the direct market.

The sensitivity of mortgage loans to variations in market rates can be examined with the aid of the flow-of-funds model mentioned earlier.[9] First, if portfolio earnings are sufficient to allow a rise in deposit rate ceilings equal to the rise in market rates, results from the model suggest that deposit rates will go up over a two-year period by a nearly matching amount. Except for an increase in life insurance policy loans, the loss of funds by the mortgage lending institutions is small. A drop in mortgage loans, equal to less than 2 percent of the outstanding stock after three years, is not the result of a gain of one percentage point in market rates, but occurs primarily because the mortgage rate does not rise proportionately to the rise in other rates and the institutions shift their portfolios toward other investments.

On the other hand, if deposit rates are constrained by rate ceilings or by insufficient portfolio earnings, the loss of deposit funds is far more substantial; as a result, the stock of mortgage loans declines by more than 6 percent in response to a one percentage point rise in market interest rates.

For the rest of this decade a level of market rates two percentage points higher could not be matched by the deposit rate. If we assume that deposit rate ceilings are raised in step with the rise of portfolio income, the deposit rate increases would average less than half of the increase in market rates. As a result, the stock of mortgages would be $40 billion to $75 billion below the projected levels, and the housing goals outlined in chapter 2 could not be met without far higher levels of government support than we have assumed.

It is, however, easy to exaggerate the effects of inflation on the capital markets: its role in increasing the dollar volume of borrowing always seems more obvious than the accompanying rise in savings. If we had worked out a detailed capital market projection, the numbers would all be bigger; the Federal Reserve would have to accommodate a more rapid expansion of the money supply; and nominal interest rates would be higher. But except for the transitional problems of the financial intermediaries the long-term implications are minor. The real difficulties for the capital markets come from sudden changes in the rate of inflation and nominal interest rates. A system that relies heavily on supplying savers

9. Bosworth and Duesenberry, "A Flow of Funds Model." For the simulations reported here, we have suppressed all responses of expenditures to credit market changes and deal only with the credit market adjustments.

with highly liquid short-term claims and borrowers with long-term fixed liabilities does not easily withstand jolts.

Oil and the Foreign Balance

Our projections for the balance of payments incorporate the price effects on U.S. imports of the higher cost of oil, but they do not fully reflect some of the issues raised by the oil exporting countries' rapid accumulation of financial assets. The real resource costs of the sharp rise in oil prices are relatively small for the industrial countries. For example, U.S. oil imports were expected to rise by $16 billion in 1974, which, as a share of GNP, is not an intolerable shift of resources. Even for a country such as Japan that is more dependent on imported oil, the cost increases do not represent a severe drop in living standards.

Furthermore, over the next few years the loss of real resources is far less than the numbers imply. Imports of goods and services by the oil exporting countries will not match the increase in export revenue. Thus the exporting countries will accumulate financial claims against the importing countries, and the transfer of real resources will be only a fraction of their export revenue. How this large pool of financial assets will be managed, however, is of concern to U.S. capital markets.

The higher relative price of oil is the major reason that our projection of the trade surplus in 1980 is only $1 billion, although in constant 1973 (pre-embargo) prices it is $10 billion. The remaining elements of the transactions that lead to foreign purchases of U.S. financial assets are shown in table 3-8. This approach of beginning with a trade balance and deriving compensating capital flows is well suited to a world of fixed exchange rates. With flexible exchange rates, however, it is also useful to examine the problem from the capital market side and derive the adjustments in exchange rates and trade flows necessary to achieve a balance for foreign accounts.

Estimates of the trade surplus of the oil exporting countries for 1974 have ranged from $50 billion to $70 billion. Although the expanded import capacity of these countries and the stimulus to develop substitutes for oil may offset some growth in world demand in future years, the cumulative trade surplus at current relative oil prices could approach $500 billion by 1980. Thus other countries, as a whole, will be running a large

Table 3-8. *Sources and Uses of Foreign Claims on the United States, Selected Periods, 1961–80*

Billions of dollars, average annual flows

Source or use	1961–65	1966–70	1971–73	1974–80[a]
U.S. payments to foreigners				
Net exports of goods and services (sign reversed)	−6.4	−3.7	−0.3	−2.0
Personal and government transfers	2.7	3.0	3.6	4.4
U.S. direct investment abroad[b]	2.2	2.5	2.4	1.5
Foreign borrowing in U.S. credit markets[c]	2.0	1.2	3.5	3.6
Change in U.S. official reserve assets	−0.8	−0.4	−1.3	0.0
U.S. government loans to foreigners	1.2	1.7	1.8	0.5
Sources, total	0.9	4.3	9.7	8.0
Allocation of foreign claims on U.S.				
Demand and time deposits	1.1	0.5	3.0	3.0
Bank liabilities to foreign affiliates	0.2	1.4	−0.7	0.0
Direct investment in U.S.	0.1	0.5	0.8	1.5
Investment in U.S. credit markets	0.7	3.1	14.2	5.0
Unallocated assets and statistical discrepancy (net)	−1.2	−1.2	−7.6	−1.5
Uses, total	0.9	4.3	9.7	8.0

Sources: See the appendix.
a. Projected.
b. Net of U.S. security issues abroad to finance U.S. investment abroad.
c. Includes bank loans.

trade deficit in future years and the total of the financial assets available for reinvestment will become extremely large. These two developments will require some compensating policy adjustments.

The assessment of what constitutes a desirable trade balance has changed considerably. In the past the industrial countries averaged a small surplus equal to the amount of capital flows to the developing countries. The prescribed responses to deficits were devaluation and domestic deflation. But in the future such policies will only shift the burden among the oil importing countries and invite retaliatory measures. The industrial countries will have to accept substantial trade account deficits, since normal corrective measures cannot eliminate the trade deficit of the group as a whole in relation to the oil exporting countries.

The means to finance the deficits are the trade surpluses of the oil exporting countries, but it is unlikely that the pattern of their financial investment will correspond to the deficits of importing countries, and some redistribution of financial flows must take place. Such redistribution would involve the Eurocurrency markets, new international institutions, and U.S. capital markets.

With an estimated net size of $150 billion at the end of 1973, the Eurocurrency market has demonstrated the ability to absorb a large influx of new funds. Much of the initial surplus is being channeled through this market. However, it is primarily a market for short-term liquid funds whereas the needs of the deficit countries are for long- or medium-term obligations. Private institutions are not in a position to arbitrage the risks of individual countries' credit policies to the extent that may be required. There are also risks of short-term instability arising from sudden shifts of these funds among countries.

Another approach to the refinancing problems would be to use an organization such as the International Monetary Fund as a financial intermediary. This could provide a better guarantee to lenders than investment in individual national markets and also a means of lengthening the maturity of the debt. But such a system implies a degree of control by the international agency that individual deficit countries might be unwilling to accept.

If left to the private market because of an inability to reach formal agreement, a significant portion of the oil surplus will probably flow through the U.S. capital markets. At present, the United States has the world's most highly developed long-term markets, which might thus become a major financial intermediary for the surplus. If all countries agreed to accept their oil deficits, the capital inflow into the United States would be offset by an equal outflow of private and official loans to other deficit countries. Although this would have little effect on resource allocation in the United States, some changes would be required in its monetary policy to ensure that sudden shifts in inflows and outflows were not allowed to disrupt the private economy. On a large scale such intermediation would mean a closer integration of U.S. and foreign capital markets and a changed role for domestic monetary policy. Restrictive policy, for example, would result in larger capital inflows and smaller interest rate increases than previously. The restraint would operate through a compensating reduction of net exports, resulting from exchange rate increases rather than from the direct effect on private demand. The trade balance would thus become a more significant mechanism for the transmission of monetary policy changes to the real sector.

In practice, however, it will prove difficult to define the appropriate balance-of-payments deficit for an oil importing country. The volume of U.S. lending to foreigners is unlikely to offset the capital inflows precisely. The result will be a change in exchange rates and in the U.S. trade balance. Some countries may continue to view a trade surplus as necessary for stimulating domestic employment, and may restrain their foreign borrowing in an attempt to shift their trade deficit to the United States. Such a move could cause political problems and a revival of protectionism in this country. For our purposes, a shift of the federal budget toward a greater deficit would be necessary to offset the deflationary effects of a trade deficit. In effect, the availability of resources for domestic purposes would be increased at the cost of larger future foreign debt repayments. Alternatively, in a world of rapid inflation governments could become increasingly concerned about the effects of devaluation on domestic prices, and might use the oil deficit as an excuse for heavy foreign borrowing, thus stimulating U.S. exports and requiring a more restrictive fiscal position.

All of these issues are very uncertain at present. It is not clear that the current high price for oil can be maintained. But even if it is, the dominant problem seems to be in the financial area rather than in that of real resource transfers. What constitutes a desirable trade balance needs to be reinterpreted. As the oil importing countries are forced to accept trade deficits, the danger of competitive devaluations for the purpose of shifting the deficit to others arises. And the impact for these countries is similar to government tax increases in the restrictive effect on domestic demand. Compensating adjustments such as shifting the government budget toward a larger deficit may be necessary. The financial adjustments appear to be manageable, but they will require a degree of international cooperation that has been difficult to achieve in past years.

Conclusion

Long-term economic forecasting is a notoriously inaccurate undertaking. As the recent unexpected shortages in fuel and some foodstuffs (with commensurate price rises) have demonstrated, long-term projections cannot hope to take into account periodic surprises. Yet each time the economy has had these jolts, it has paid the costs of ignoring the future implications of current policy decisions. The long lead times involved in many capital expenditure decisions dictate that we at least attempt to examine some of their consequences.

The results of this study suggest that the size of future capital needs—while large—is not unmanageable when put in the context of a growing economy with an increased capacity to supply savings for investment. Our projections include a large number of costly programs in energy production, pollution abatement, mass transportation, housing, and raw material processing. But offsetting reductions in needs can be anticipated in other areas. The end of the postwar "baby boom" has already begun to slow the growth of expenditures for education; the interstate highway program is nearing completion; and in the private sector a slower expansion of demand will reduce capital needs in the consumer goods industries. If all the objectives are met, the share of total output devoted to private investment will rise to about 16 percent in 1980. Although this is above the average of the 1960s, it is similar to that of the 1950s and the year 1973.

There is, of course, much uncertainty connected with the estimates of capital needs for the remainder of the decade. The difficulties are increased because levels of both private saving and investment must be projected before any conclusions about government policies can be derived. In contrast to our estimates of capital needs, those of private saving could be characterized as conservative. The rise in the personal saving rate over the last decade is not projected to continue, and only a modest rise in the share of output going to profits is anticipated. Despite these biases, investment needs are found to be only slightly in excess of private saving.

The major conclusion for stabilization policy is that a significant shift toward larger government budget surpluses and an easier monetary policy is needed. If the economy were to achieve a 4 percent unemployment rate by 1980, the required federal surplus—needed to fill the gap between private investment and private savings—would amount to about half of 1 percent of GNP. This surplus would have to be much larger if it became necessary to restrain private demand to lower rates of resource utilization because of inflationary pressures.

In the financial sector significant problems in transferring income claims between savers and investors are anticipated only under conditions of a relatively restrictive monetary policy. Most of the growth of financial claims is associated with heavy business borrowing needs and a rapid growth of residential mortgages. State and local governments' borrowing will moderate slightly and public holdings of federal debt will decline if a budget surplus is achieved. Since business and mortgage borrowing are primarily long term, financial intermediaries will play an important role. In general, this type of illiquid debt is not attractive to the household sector. Financial intermediaries reconcile the disparate preferences of lenders and borrowers by issuing liquid short-term liabilities and purchasing long-term assets. However, a sharp rise of market rates severely limits the ability of the institutions to attract funds for long-term mortgage lending. Thus the housing goals used in this study could not be achieved under conditions of rising market interest rates. In addition, a slow growth of bank reserves would prevent commercial banks from financing the projected level of business lending.

The projections also indicate that the reduced volume of federal securities might result in a shortage of highly liquid marketable financial assets, which might mean a rapid expansion in the demand for negotiable certificates of deposit as a substitute instrument.

Finally, the large trade deficit of the developed countries resulting from the sharp increase in oil prices may continue for the rest of the decade. It may become necessary for the United States to maintain a large trade deficit to provide an orderly refinancing of the oil countries' surpluses. In such a situation the higher level of imports than of exports would exert a considerable depressive influence on the U.S. economy. As a result, the appropriate federal budget surplus would be much smaller and a larger portion of the capital financing needs would be met by foreign capital inflows.

It should be kept in mind that this study is based on an assumed rapid return to low levels of unemployment in the United States. Certainly, our conclusions about a federal budget surplus are irrelevant to the current situation of substantial unused resources. At present, a rise in output of investment goods does not require offsetting demand reductions in other areas. On the other hand, our conclusion of no serious future capital shortages would not apply if a very rapid expansion of total demand in future years did not allow adequate time for new capital facilities to be constructed and put in place.

Sources of Data
for the Tables in Chapter 3

THIS APPENDIX provides the sources for the tables in chapter 3 preceded by a key to the abbreviations used to identify the sources.

Abbreviation and Source

FoF, 1945–72; Board of Governors of the Federal Reserve System,
FoF, 1973 "Flow of Funds Accounts, 1945–1972" (1973; processed), and "Flow of Funds, Unadjusted, 4th Quarter, 1973, Preliminary" (February 8, 1974; processed), respectively. For these two sources, the abbreviation is followed by the name of the FoF table in the source and the appropriate line number from that table.

SCB, Nov. 71 Allan H. Young, John C. Musgrave, and Claudia Harkins, "Residential Capital in the United States, 1925–70," *Survey of Current Business,* vol. 51 (November 1971), pp. 16–28.

SCB, Feb. 73 *Survey of Current Business,* "Government Gross Fixed Capital Formation," vol. 53 (February 1973), pp. 7–9.

SCB, Feb. 74 *Survey of Current Business,* vol. 54 (February 1974).

HUD, 1971 U.S. Department of Housing and Urban Development, *1971 HUD Statistical Yearbook* (1972).

U.S. Budget   *Special Analyses, Budget of the United States Government, Fiscal Year 1975,* "Special Analyses D," and comparable analyses in relevant preceding issues.

FRB   *Federal Reserve Bulletin,* vol. 60 (1974), and preceding issues, where relevant.

FRBB   Barry Bosworth and James S. Duesenberry, "A Flow of Funds Model and Its Implications," in *Issues in Federal Debt Management,* Proceedings of a Conference held by the Federal Reserve Bank of Boston, June 1973.

Table Sources

Table 3-1   *Value of residential real estate:* SCB, Nov. 71; HUD, 1971.
    Debt-to-value ratio: This table, ratio of line 3 to line 1.
    Value of residential mortgage stock: FoF, 1945–72, and FoF, 1973, "Home Mortgages," line 1, plus "Multi-family Residential Mortgages," line 1.

Table 3-2   *Gross capital formation:* SCB, Feb. 73.
    Federal capital grants: Constructed from data in U.S. Budget.
    Bond issues: FRB (May 1974), p. A 41, total under "issues for new capital," and preceding FRBs.
    Other financing: Residual (this table, line 1 minus lines 2 and 3).
    Outstanding debt, long-term and *short-term:* FoF, 1945–72, and FoF, 1973, "State and Local Government Securities," lines 1, 3, and 2, respectively.

Table 3-3   *Total business investment:* FoF, 1945–72, "Income and Product Accounts: GNP Expenditures and Gross Saving," line 7 minus line 11, plus "Nonfinancial Corporate Business," line 27; and comparable data for 1973 from SCB, Feb. 74, tables 11 and 15, pp. 12, 13.
    Internal financing: FoF, 1945–72, "Income and Product Accounts: GNP Expenditures and Gross Saving," line 53 plus line 61 minus line 62; comparable data for 1973 from SCB, Feb. 74, tables 4 and 6, p. 11; and data on capital

consumption of owner-occupied homes provided by the U.S. Bureau of Economic Analysis.

External financing needed: This table, difference between lines 1 and 2.

Corporate bonds: FoF, 1945–72, and FoF, 1973, "Corporate and Foreign Bonds," line 1 minus lines 3 and 6.

Corporate stock: FoF, 1945–72, and FoF, 1973, "Corporate Equities," line 4 plus line 7.

Commercial mortgages: FoF, 1945–72, and FoF, 1973, "Commercial Mortgages," line 1.

Residential mortgages: FoF, 1945–72, and FoF, 1973, "Home Mortgages," line 3 plus line 4, plus "Multi-family Residential Mortgages," line 1.

Bank loans: FoF, 1945–72, and FoF, 1973, "Bank Loans Not Elsewhere Classified," summation of lines 13, 14, 15, 19, 20.

Open-market paper: FoF, 1945–72, and FoF, 1973, "Open-Market Paper," line 2 minus line 5 plus line 6 minus line 10 plus line 12.

Liquid assets: FoF, 1945–72, "Nonfinancial Corporate Business," line 17, plus "Finance Companies," line 2; FoF, 1973, "Corporate Business," line 18, plus "Finance Companies," line 2.

Consumer credit assets: FoF, 1945–72, and FoF, 1973, "Consumer Credit," summation of lines 6, 7, 10, 12, 13.

Residual assets: This table, external funds raised minus external financing needed, minus liquid and consumer credit assets.

Table 3-4 *Budget deficit:* FoF, 1945–72, and FoF, 1973, "U.S. Government," line 11 (sign reversed).

Federal Home Loan Bank advances to savings and loan associations: FoF, 1945–72, and FoF, 1973, "Federally Sponsored Credit Agencies," line 11.

Residential mortgages of Federal National Mortgage Association and other agencies: FoF, 1945–72, and FoF, 1973, "U.S. Government," line 19, plus "Federally Sponsored Credit Agencies," line 6.

Official foreign reserve assets: FoF, 1945–72, and FoF, 1973, "Gold and Official Foreign Exchange Holdings," line 1.

Loans to foreigners: FoF, 1945–72, and FoF, 1973, "Other Types" (of other loans), line 11.

Other loans and adjustments: Residual (this table, total liabilities minus budget deficit, minus the assets listed above).

Unborrowed reserves: FRB (February 1974), p. 94, and preceding issues.

Currency: FRB (February 1974), p. 90, and preceding issues.

Credit market debt: FoF, 1945–72, and FoF, 1973, "U.S. Government Securities Market Summary," line 15 plus line 18.

Table 3-5 ISSUERS OF CREDIT

Federal government: Table 3-4 above, credit market debt.

Nonfinancial business: Table 3-3 above, long-term plus short-term external funds raised, minus residential mortgages.

State and local governments: Calculated from table 3-2 above, outstanding debt.

Foreign investors: Table 3-8 above, foreign borrowing in U.S. credit markets.

Commercial banks: FoF, 1945–72, "Commercial Banks," line 37 plus line 38, plus "Domestic Affiliates of Commercial Banks," line 5; FoF, 1973, "Commercial Banks," line 30 plus line 31, plus "Domestic Affiliates of Commercial Banks," line 5.

HOLDERS OF CREDIT

Commercial banks: FoF, 1945–72, and FoF, 1973, "Commercial Banks," lines 6 plus 10 plus 11 plus 17, plus "Commercial Mortgages," line 9, plus "Bank Loans Not Elsewhere Classified," line 16, plus bank loans from table 3-3 above.

Nonbank intermediaries: FoF, 1945–72, and FoF, 1973, "Savings and Loan Associations," line 5, plus "Mutual Savings Banks," lines 5 plus 7 plus 8 plus 9, plus "Life

Insurance Companies," lines 5 plus 7 plus 8 plus 9, plus "Commercial Mortgages," lines 10 plus 13.

Nonfinancial business: FoF, 1945–72, "Nonfinancial Corporate Business," lines 21 plus 22 plus 23 plus 24, and FoF, 1973, same table, lines 22 through 25.

State and local governments: FoF, 1945–72, "State and Local Governments—General Funds," line 13 minus line 18, and FoF, 1973, same table, line 16 minus line 21.

Foreign investors: Table 3-8 below, investment in U.S. credit markets.

Households and others: Residual (issuers of credit, total, minus holders of credit, total for the other five sectors in this table).

Table 3-6 COMMERCIAL BANKS

Deposit accounts: FoF, 1945–72, and FoF, 1973, "Commercial Banks," line 27, plus the change in the monthly average of currency and demand deposits for December of the relevant years, from FRB (February 1974), p. 90, and preceding issues.

Residential mortgages: FoF, 1945–72, and FoF, 1973, "Home Mortgages," line 12, plus "Multi-family Residential Mortgages," line 9.

Credit market holdings: Table 3-5 above, commercial banks (holders of credit).

Consumer credit: FoF, 1945–72, and FoF, 1973, "Consumer Credit," line 8 plus line 14, plus "Bank Loans Not Elsewhere Classified," line 12.

SAVINGS AND LOAN ASSOCIATIONS

Deposit accounts: FoF, 1945–72, and FoF, 1973, "Savings and Loan Associations," line 11.

Residential mortgages: FoF, 1945–72, and FoF, 1973, "Home Mortgages," line 14, plus "Multi-family Residential Mortgages," line 11.

Credit market holdings: Same as the savings and loan associations' portion of nonbank intermediaries in table 3-5 above.

MUTUAL SAVINGS BANKS

Deposit accounts: FoF, 1945–72, "Mutual Savings Banks," line 15, and FoF, 1973, same table, line 16.

Residential mortgages: FoF, 1945–72, and FoF, 1973, "Home Mortgages," line 15, plus "Multi-family Residential Mortgages," line 12.

Credit market holdings: Same as the mutual savings banks' portion of nonbank intermediaries in table 3-5 above.

LIFE INSURANCE COMPANIES

Reserves: FoF, 1945–72, and FoF, 1973, "Life Insurance Companies," line 15 plus line 16, minus "Other Types" (of other loans), line 18.

Residential mortgages: FoF, 1945–72, and FoF, 1973, "Home Mortgages," line 18, plus "Multi-family Residential Mortgages," line 13.

Credit market holdings: FoF, 1945–72, and FoF, 1973, "Life Insurance Companies," lines 5 plus 7 plus 8 plus 9, plus "Open-Market Paper," line 23 (line 27 in FoF, 1973).

ADDENDA

Residential mortgages, total: Derived from table 3-1 above.

Federal Home Loan Bank advances: Table 3-4 above.

Federal National Mortgage Association purchases of residential mortgages: FoF, 1945–72, and FoF, 1973, "Federally Sponsored Credit Agencies," line 6.

Table 3-7   Calculated from FRBB, tables 2.1, 3.1, pp. 88, 94.

Table 3-8   *Net exports* and *Personal and government transfers:* FoF, 1945–72, and FoF, 1973, "Rest of the World," lines 1 and 4, respectively.

U.S. direct investment abroad: FoF, 1945–72, "Rest of the World," line 32, and FoF, 1973, same table, line 34.

Foreign borrowing in U.S. credit markets: FoF, 1945–72, "Rest of the World," lines 23 plus 25 plus 26, plus "Open-Market Paper," line 15, and FoF, 1973, "Rest of the World," lines 24 plus 26 plus 27, plus "Open-Market Paper," line 15.

Change in U.S. official reserve assets and *U.S. government loans to foreigners:* Table 3-4 above.

Demand and time deposits: FoF, 1945–72, and FoF, 1973, "Rest of the World," line 9 plus line 10.

Bank liabilities to foreign affiliates: FoF, 1945–72, "Rest of the World," line 18, and FoF, 1973, same table, line 19.

Direct investment in U.S.: FoF, 1945–72, "Rest of the World," line 19, and FoF, 1973, same table, line 20.

Investment in U.S. credit markets: FoF, 1945–72, and FoF, 1973, "Rest of the World," line 11 plus line 12.

Unallocated assets and statistical discrepancy: Residual (this table, sources, total, minus summation of the four items above for net foreign accumulation of claims on U.S.).

capital
needs
in the
seventies

Barry Bosworth, James S. Duesenberry, *and* Andrew S. Carron

In recent years, as interest rates and credit restraints have fluctuated widely, the performance of capital markets has been of growing concern. Current market structure has placed certain types of socially valuable investment at a competitive disadvantage—housing and state and local government construction are prime examples. Many doubt that the rising demand for capital to find new sources of energy, to curb pollution, and to build houses, create jobs, and provide mass transit can be met.

The authors of this study project for the rest of this decade the likely magnitude of capital supply and demand, presenting a range of estimates for the major investment sectors and for the whole economy at alternative unemployment and inflation rates. They discuss the effect on capital markets of changes in federal regulations and programs—for example, changes in deposit rate ceilings and government purchase of mortgages—and of monetary and fiscal policy.

The projections suggest that the size of future capital needs, though large, is not unmanageable. While some of the newer programs are costly, there will be offsetting reductions in others, such as education and the interstate highway program; demand for consumer goods will expand more slowly than in the past, reducing the need of these industries for capital. But in the authors' view, when the economy is operating at high levels of employment, a shift toward larger budget surpluses than those achieved in the past must be made to stimulate the economy and to avoid future shortages of capital.

Barry Bosworth is a research associate in the Brookings Economic Studies program; James S. Duesenberry is a professor of economics at Harvard University and a member of the Brookings associated staff; and Andrew S. Carron, a former Brookings research assistant, is now on the staff of Senator Thomas Eagleton.

The Brookings Institution • Washington, D. C.

Cover Design: Carol Crosby Black